Do you remember eagerly anticipating a visit with Santa? Christmas cookies fresh from the oven? Twinkling lights and evergreen wreaths? A Christmas tree towering to the ceiling? Home and family again loom large in *Merry Christmas from a Little Town Called Paxton,* the newest book from Donna and Pat DeMuth. With their ever merry and oh-so-slightly wistful style of tale-spinning, the DeMuth sisters once more take us on a journey of reminiscence to a time of innocence. An absolute must-read, every page of *Merry Christmas from a Little Town Called Paxton* brings to life for the reader a hometown sparkling with the joy and wonder of that greatest of holidays. A more-than-worthy follow-up to *In a Little Town Called Paxton, Merry Christmas from a Little Town Called Paxton* left me eager in anticipation, myself, for the third Paxton book. Please, Santa, would you bring me more stories from this wondrous duo?

—Shawn T Bean, editor

Merry Christmas from a Little Town Called Paxton

With best wishes
Pat DeMuth
Donna DeMuth

Also by Donna and Patricia DeMuth

* * *

In a Little Town Called Paxton

Is burning down the garage really the best way to enliven a boring Saturday afternoon? Is it possible to cut your contributions to the church by 75% without incurring divine retribution? How do you reinstate rationality when military thinking goes out of control? Can you effectively dispose of a bucket of dirty scrub water by throwing it out the window? Can you ban puberty? Most importantly, how do you do all of this when you are under the age of twelve? Find all the answers and much more in a little town called Paxton.

    A closely-knit family living in a small, rural community during the 1950's and '60's provides the setting for this delightful collection of stories. With gentle humor, the authors take you along as they revisit their childhood and share some of the trials and joys of growing up. By the time you turn the last page, you will be eagerly looking forward to another visit.

Merry Christmas from a Little Town Called Paxton

Donna R. DeMuth
and
Patricia J. DeMuth

Illustrations by
Caressa B. Bean

iUniverse, Inc.
New York Lincoln Shanghai

Merry Christmas from a Little Town Called Paxton

Copyright © 2005 by Donna R. DeMuth and Patricia J. DeMuth

All rights reserved. No part of this book may be used or reproduced by any means, graphic, electronic, or mechanical, including photocopying, recording, taping or by any information storage retrieval system without the written permission of the publisher except in the case of brief quotations embodied in critical articles and reviews.

iUniverse books may be ordered through booksellers or by contacting:

iUniverse
2021 Pine Lake Road, Suite 100
Lincoln, NE 68512
www.iuniverse.com
1-800-Authors (1-800-288-4677)

ISBN-13: 978-0-595-37295-9 (pbk)
ISBN-13: 978-0-595-81693-4 (ebk)
ISBN-10: 0-595-37295-3 (pbk)
ISBN-10: 0-595-81693-2 (ebk)

Printed in the United States of America

Dedicated to our children: Donna's daughter, Shelly (Crosthwait) Cathey, and Pat's two sons, Shawn and Jody Bean. Each of you has contributed immeasurably to our lives, and we love you dearly.

Since this book is centered on Christmas, our thoughts naturally turned to you and the many wonderful holidays we have spent together over the years. We have been delighted to see each of you embrace the traditions of our family, and we have been charmed by your own unique additions to them:

Shelly, who has become the family's Christmas Princess, and has raised the making and sharing of Christmas cookies to the level of an art.

Shawn, who has spiced the traditional with modern technology to produce a new magic for the holidays.

Jody, the guru of Christmas cards, who always manages to find unique, timely, pertinent and hilarious cards to convey his holiday greetings.

It warms our hearts to see all of you carrying on so many of the traditions your grandmother taught you. Merry Christmas, everyone!

Contents

Some Background..1
A Jolly Old Elf 7
Buy a Wreath, Jeanette Isabella..................................15
Oh What Fun It Is To Ride In A Four-Door Chevrolet...........27
'Tis the Season 41
Christmas Is Coming, One Of the Kids Is Getting Fat?...........49
Hey, St. Jude..59
And a Chicken in a Pear Tree......................................71
If You Haven't Got a Ha'penny, Then God Bless You...........79
Just Close Your Eyes and Click Your Heels.................87
Do You See What I See?..99
O Tannenbaum..107
The Red Coat 113
Away From the Manger 119
The Holly and the Tin Foil?..123
'Til Next Time..133

Acknowledgments

Christmas is the most meaningful holiday of the year for us, as we are sure it is for the majority of you, our readers. We had a lot of fun writing these stories, and the task just seemed to flow from our fingertips. Again, we were supported, encouraged and applauded by many friends and family members whom we want to take the time to acknowledge and thank.

First of all, Judy Morrill, dearest of friends for over thirty years, and a person who thoroughly understands that being "politically correct" about Christmas is the biggest humbug of all. Thank you, Judy, for being there, for being you, and for being a consistent point of sanity in this insane world.

Recognition is also due to Dennis Gallagher and Connie Harrison, who turned into such an enthusiastic two-person sales crew for our first book, and have been bugging us constantly for the second one. Okay, guys, here it is.

Once again, another huge thanks to our brother (and "test guinea pig"), Ray DeMuth. Ray is our first reader and critic for our stories, he is a continual source of encouragement, and has become our unofficial "California Guru." He keeps telling us, "If you are doing what you are meant to do, the path will open for you, and things will come together and happen."

Thanks to our aunt, Sister Leonardine Sconzert, for all of her support and prayers, even if she did think it hilarious that the Christmas "miracle" landed Donna facedown in the snow.

Shawn Bean did another incredible job of editing, gently offering corrections with a touch of humor and, at all times, keeping criticism positive and truly constructive. He is also responsible for several of the chapter titles.

While searching for an illustrator, we received an early Christmas surprise of our own. Checking our email one evening, we found that one of Shawn's messages to us had an attachment. When we opened it, we found a picture that perfectly complemented one of our stories. Pat's fourteen-year-old granddaughter, Caressa, knew of our search and took it upon herself to submit some sketches for consideration. Caressa Bean, a budding artist in the family, did all the pictures in this book.

In some of the stories, names have been changed to avoid possible embarrassment. For instance, you won't find a "Parkerville, Illinois" on any map, but there is a small town out among the cornfields where the events happened as described. We plan to take the secret to our graves.

Finally, a huge thanks to all of the readers who have given us such positive feedback on our first book, and who tell us they are eagerly awaiting our second one. We hope you enjoy this book even more.

"I have always thought of Christmas as a good time: a forgiving, charitable, pleasant time: the only time I know of when men and women seem to open their shut-up hearts freely."

Charles Dickens, *A Christmas Carol*

Some Background...

Christmas—as the song says, "It's the most wonderful time of the year." Christmas should be a time of good feelings, friendship, and wonderful memories. It should be a time when we *take* the time to make the world a better and more magical place.

During the Christmas season, our hometown of Paxton underwent a seasonal transformation. Every year, on the day after Thanksgiving, the town's Christmas tree was raised and decorated on Main Street. The following day, Santa would arrive in the annual Christmas parade. Seemingly overnight, the town prepared for this event, and when Santa showed up the downtown was bedecked with Christmas lights and decorations to welcome him. The shop windows sparkled with new displays, and the mysterious basements in the dime stores opened as once-a-year Toylands.

In the following days, the wave of Christmas spirit seemed to roll out from Main Street and wash across the town. Christmas lights, wreaths, and garlands suddenly appeared, decorating the rooflines and porches of the old Victorian homes in town. As you went down the streets, you saw that the drapes were pulled open on the large front windows of homes, each one displaying a large and beautifully decorated Christmas tree. We knew that Santa would never miss our home town on Christmas Eve: when seen from above in the dark, Paxton would appear as a small, sparkling jewel tucked into the plains of Illinois, an easy beacon for Rudolph to home in on..

Things at home underwent a seasonal shift, also. When it came to providing happiness and making things special, holidays were Mom's *forté*. She could produce magic with the stories and traditions unique to each holiday, but it was at Christmas that she truly excelled. Christmas was the biggest holiday, and every year was memorable in its own way, surrounded by the "once-a-year, *only* at Christmas" activities that Mom orchestrated.

Our Christmas season started with the beginning of Advent, and each year we refreshed our Advent wreath with new greens, ribbons, and the appropriate candles. The wreath became the centerpiece on our dining table, and remained there throughout the season. It was a wonderful timekeeper, giving us children a visual, easily understandable way to measure the time remaining until Christmas.

Attending the annual Christmas parade was a social *"must"* for us since it was the official start of the season. The rest of the holiday activities followed a set pattern and schedule: decorating the house, raising the Christmas tree, and doing the holiday baking all fell into place at their appointed times. One of the last things to be done before Christmas, usually two or three days before, was frosting and decorating the wonderful Christmas cut-out cookies made from a recipe that came from our grandmother. Mom made each activity special, and as each milestone of the season passed our anticipation and excitement grew.

Mom's wizardry even extended to something as simple as making our Christmas lists. We would each receive a gift from Mom and Dad, and we were encouraged to let them know what we wanted. To keep things manageable, however, we were each limited to a total of *three* suggestions. With that limitation in place, we each knew that we had to be very selective and use good judgment in our choices. We couldn't be willy-nilly, asking for anything and everything that struck our fancies, and we certainly didn't want to waste our "picks" on something that would become superficial or boring within a few weeks.

When the *Sears Christmas Catalog* arrived, we kids would descend on it as if it were a treasure map. We spent hours poring over the pages, carefully comparing items and marking our choices, revising our choices, and finally narrowing those choices to three items. When we finally turned our lists over to Mom, we knew that we would get one of those items, but we never knew which one it would be. We spent the final days before Christmas still in a state of excited anticipation as we tried to figure out which item on our list would be chosen. (Surprisingly enough, Santa would usually provide one of our choices, also, and somehow, he never duplicated the item that Mom and Dad chose.) The "Sears catalog game" also kept us busy and quiet for extended periods during December, giving Mom and Dad the respite and time they needed to handle the holidays. The best of it was that everyone had fun.

Some of our most treasured childhood memories center around the Christmas season, and this book is a collection of some of those stories. As in our first book, the stories are told from the perspective of children, as we remember them. We hope they add a smile and a glow to your holidays.

And so, Dear Readers, we would once again like to invite you to settle back and get comfortable, and come spend the Christmas holidays with us in a little town called Paxton.

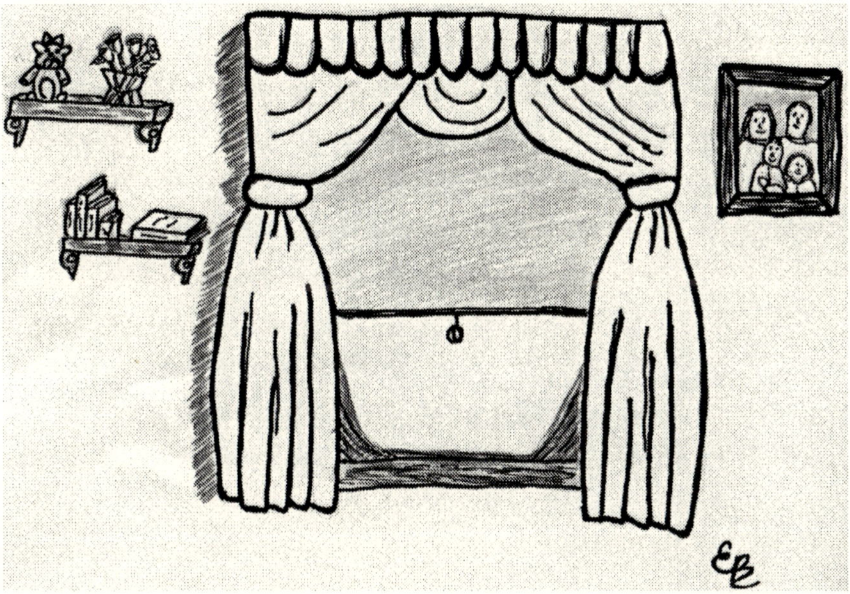

A Jolly Old Elf

...as told by Donna

Mom was waiting outside the school for me, and I was glad to see her; the day was cold and snowy—typical for December in Illinois. My three year old sister, Patty, was sitting in the front seat next to Mom, all bundled up against the weather. All you could see was her little round face and rosy cheeks. Jimmy, my older brother, wasn't in the car.

"Where's Jimmy?" I asked Mom as I crawled into the back seat.

"He's going home with Ricky, so they can work on a Cub Scout project together. Ricky's Mom will bring him home later."

"Darn! I gotta talk to him."

Mom turned around and gave me a puzzled look. "What's wrong, Donna?"

"Nuthin'," I mumbled.

The day had been pretty irritating for a six-year-old, and I didn't know how to explain my problem to my Mom. So, I sat back in the seat of the car, crossed my arms tightly across my chest, and jammed my chin down into the collar of my coat.

"Wouldn't you feel better if you talked about it?"

"No! I just wanna think."

"Okay then, I'll leave you alone while you think, but if you feel like talking, just let me know. I'm a good listener."

I looked up at my mother with relief. She wasn't going to pressure me for an explanation. Mom pulled the car away from the curb and started home. The remainder of the ride was very quiet.

My thoughts were centered on Charlie Morin. Little did I know it at that time, but Charlie would be the bane of my grade school years, and that particular day in December of 1951 was just the beginning. Oh, could I tell you stories about Charlie today! About the time he dumped a handful of baby snakes in my paper bag—or the time he tied two cats' tails together—the day he flushed my lunch down a toilet in the boys' room—and so on and so on.

Had he lied to me this time, or was he telling the truth? It was important that I get an answer to that question, and soon. It was two days before school let out for the Christmas vacation, and less than three weeks until Christmas.

When we reached the house I was still *thinking*, and had not uttered a word. I could tell that Mom was concerned, but she would just have to wait for an explanation. I took off my snowsuit (coat and pants) and other cold weather gear, and hung them on one of the pegs just inside the side door of the house. All of this was done in continued silence. After that, I marched into the dining room and up the stairs to my room. I flopped down on my bed with my mind churning. I was very worried.

My thoughts were interrupted by my Mother's voice coming from the base of the stairs, "Donna, would you like some hot tea and toast?"

"Nope. Tell Jimmy when he comes home that I gotta talk to him. Okay?"

"All right, Dear. I'm sure he'll be home soon."

Next thing I knew, my little sister was standing next to my bed, with an expectant look on her face. "Wanna play?" she asked.

"Not now. Go away!"

"Why?"

"Can't you see that I'm busy thinking?" I snapped at her. I rolled over on my side, turning my back to her.

She fled from the room, tattling as she went. "Mommy, Mommy, Donna's being mean to me."

"Oh, for Pete sakes," I thought. "She's going to drive me to an early grave!"

Before she could cause any more trouble, I hollered downstairs to my Mom. "I'm sorry. I just want to be left alone. Okay?"

I laid on my bed, mentally going over the day. No conclusions or decisions came to me. I wished Jimmy would get home—I was not blessed with an abundance of patience, and I was getting more and more frustrated.

About a zillion minutes later, I heard the back door open downstairs, and my mother's voice greeting my older brother. He was finally home! About time! I sat up on my bed to listen better. He was talking to Mom, telling her about his scout project and, in general, his day. I wished he would get done and go up to his room. I guess I could wait a little longer, but not too much longer. Finally, Jimmy came upstairs.

I waited a respectable minute and a half, and then went to his door and knocked lightly.

"Come in, Donna," he allowed.

He was standing by his bedroom window, watching the snow that had started about a half hour before, come down gently as it re-blanketed the front yard. I went up and stood beside him. I didn't start the conversation—I waited for him to do that.

"What's buggin' you? Mom said you wanted to talk to me."

"Do just babies believe in Santa Claus?"

He turned his head to me with a puzzled look on his face. "What? Better start at the beginning."

"Well, Charlie Morin said that there isn't a real Santa Claus, and that your Mom and Dad pretend to be Santa, and that only babies believe in Santa Claus. I told him that wasn't true. There was a real Santa Claus, and he was just making that up about Mom and Dad. He called me a 'baby' all day long, and some of the other kids did too. Do you believe in Santa?"

"Why would he do that?" Jim asked.

"Because he's mean! He picks on me all the time."

"Why?"

"He says he loves me and he is going to marry me some day. He also calls me his *girlfriend*."

"He's got a funny way of showing that."

"I don't care about that and his silly ways! I just want to know if what he said is true!"

"Okay, just settle down. Maybe he was talking about the Santa in the Christmas parade, or the one that shows up at the Christmas party at church. You know they aren't the real Santa, but folks' Dads who are helping the real Santa out. He can't be in a hundred towns on the same day, so he has other people play Santa for him."

"Yeah, I know that. But, does the real Santa come by our house on Christmas Eve?"

"I'm not 100 percent sure, but I think he does. Where would Mom and Dad get all those toys, and who eats all the cookies?"

I was silent for a minute or two. "But, Jimmy, how can we know for sure?"

"Is it that important to you?"

"Yes! I don't want Mom and Dad to have to spend lots of money on toys and stuff. Those things should come from Santa. Besides, Dad isn't even here this year, and Mom would have to do everything by herself." (Our father, who was in the Air Force, was on an eighteen month tour of duty in Alaska, and would not be home that Christmas.)

Jim paused for a second, and then turned to me and said, "Tell you what—I want you to forget about what Charlie Morin said for now. I'll talk to Mom and let you know what she says. I bet she comes up with an answer. Is it a deal?"

"Okay. I'll wait 'til you talk to her. But, I still hate Charlie."

*   *   *

Even though our Dad was temporarily absent, things did not change their daily routine. Every evening we sat down together, as a family, and had our dinner. Dad's place was unoccupied, waiting for him to return. This was the time of day we could tell our daily stories, ask questions we had for our parents, or converse in general. It was an uninterrupted time during which we could cement our family bonds to each other. If Mom had received a letter that day from Dad, at the end of the meal she would read it to all of us before we left the table (all of the letter, that is, except the mushy stuff Dad wrote just to her). If we wanted, we could also write Dad a small letter back, and she would enclose it with the letter she wrote to him that night after we went to bed. Sometimes Dad would answer our letters individually, and then we would receive a *real* letter in the *real* mail just for us!

That evening the conversation quickly turned to Christmas, since it was so imminent. We talked about the up-coming Christmas parties, when we were going to frost the cookies, and what size tree we would be able to buy that year. Every now and then, one of us would impatiently start talking while someone else was speaking, and Mom always interrupted our interruption, and said, "Wait, wait, I'm all confused now. Who was talking first, who was second, and who was third?" This comment would pause all of us, quiet any too loud voice, and/or stop an on-coming argument. She was a genius when it came to handling children!

When we finished our meal, before we children scrambled away from the table, Mom brought up my problem about Santa Claus. (It surprised me a little that she mentioned what Charlie had said in front of my little sister, Patty. But that concern straightened itself quickly.)

"So, what do you think, Donna? Is there or isn't there a Santa Claus?" she asked me.

Before I answered Mom's question, I looked over at Patty. She was sitting there, staring at me with those big round blue eyes of hers with her mouth hanging open. I wasn't sure what to say!

"Ah, I-I-I, I think so, but now I'm not so sure." (Pat swung her head towards Mom with the same incredible look on her face.)

Gawd Almighty, the trouble Charlie had caused was now spreading! Why doesn't Mom just say there is a Santa Claus, and let that be that? *"Because you wouldn't accept that as an answer,"* a little voice said in my head.

Pat's head swung back to me, but now her little bottom lip was starting to tremble.

"Oh, no," I thought. "How am I going to get out of this mess! And, would someone put a paper bag over my sister's head so that I don't have to look at that pitiful little face!"

Before I could say anything further, Mom asked, "You believed in Santa Claus yesterday, didn't you, Donna?" (I nodded my head yes) "But, today, because Charlie says you are wrong, you have stopped believing."

"I didn't say I don't believe today, I just said I'm not sure I believe!" I splurted out.

"Let's think about this for a minute," Mom said. "Why would Charlie be right, and you would be wrong?"

"I don't know! He sounded so sure, and he laughed at me! And, I'm so confused! And, why would he be so mean?"

"Okay, let's play make believe for a minute, and say Charlie is right and there isn't a Santa Claus." (Patty made an audible hiccough sound.) "Remember, we are playing make believe," Mom reiterated.

"On Christmas Eve we will go to Midnight Mass like we always do. The church will be decorated with lights and Christmas flowers, the candles burning, and the big nativity set up at the front of the altar waiting for the baby Jesus. Everyone will be dressed up in their best clothes, and wishing each other a "Merry Christmas." Before and during mass we will all be singing the best Christmas carols we know, feeling very happy and peaceful towards all. Can you see all of this?" We all nodded our heads.

Mom continued, "Then, on Christmas day we will get up early, the tree will be all lit up, there will be plates of cookies, bowls of nuts and candy, and the presents under the tree will be only those we got for each other. After we open our presents and munch on goodies, we will have a big, yummy Christmas dinner, and eat 'til we are stuffed. All of this with no Santa."

"Would that be so terrible? Would that be an awful Christmas?" Mom asked.

We all shook our heads "no," and giggled a little.

"Every Christmas you can remember until now, Santa has visited our house and left presents for everyone. Right? And, those presents brought a lot of happiness to each of us. And, we would miss Santa if he was not around on Christmas. Nevertheless, Christmas would still be a wonderful day full of love and very good things. I'm sure all of us want it to be the same this year. I'm sure Santa wants that too, and I'm sure you also want that, Donna. It's very important that you believe in that wonderful day to share and give the happiness. You have always been a big part of everyone's Christmas, and we don't want that to change. We want you to believe in Christmas with us, and forget the little bit of bad news Charlie had to add to our holiday. Do you think you can do that?"

"Yes!" I said with enthusiasm and confidence. "I can! Phooey on Charlie!"

Everyone repeated "phooey on Charlie" too. I could finally look straight at Patty, and, even though her eyes glistened with unshed tears, she had a big smile on her face.

* * *

Early on Christmas morning, I was awakened by Patty shaking my shoulder. "It's Christmas," she whispered in awe and anticipation. "Wake up, sleepy head."

"You go on downstairs, and I will be down shortly."

"Okay, but hurry!"

I sat up in bed and wiped my sleepy eyes. The room was bright with the morning sun, welcoming a nice day. "Oh boy, it's Christmas," I thought.

I was invigorated immediately, and jumped out of bed. I pulled on my warm bathrobe, and was ready to dash downstairs after Patty, but something stopped me short. When I had jumped out of bed, I had glanced at the window. My mind just then registered that something was different. I turned around and looked at the window again. There, etched in the frost-covered pane from outside, was a message. My mouth fell open in astonishment. The message said: *Merry Christmas, Donna.* And it was signed, *Santa.*

* * *

NOTE: Dear Reader, it would be unfair to let this story end here without a rational explanation. Several years later, my older brother and my Mom confessed that they had written the message on my window. On Christmas Eve, after I had fallen deeply asleep, Jim had crawled out of his bedroom window onto the fairly flat porch roof that was located under both bedroom windows on the front of the house. Mom had tied a thick, sturdy rope around Jim's waist as a safety line, and he carefully made his way across the roof to my window. He had etched the message in the frost with a butter knife. I must admit it was very convincing. There were even "footsteps" in the snow on the roof. It certainly added greater magic to the holiday than Charlie Morin's six-year-old cynicism did.

Buy a Wreath, Jeanette Isabella

...as told by Donna

Christmas was rapidly approaching again. I had exactly 58 cents to my name, and I was deep into my quest on how to make money. To me, one of the best parts of Christmas was buying gifts for everyone in the family. I was often hard pressed when asked what I wanted for Christmas, but I had my shopping list for others well thought out early in the season, and I needed a hell of a lot more than 58 cents.

One evening I was leisurely thumbing through one of Mom's ladies magazines, when, lo' and behold, I stumbled across the answer. I jumped up, and went to find my mother. She was in her sewing room; the perfect place to approach her with my question.

"Hey, Mom, are you busy?"

"Yes, as a matter of fact I am, Sweetheart."

Wrong answer! So, I stood behind her, not saying a word, clutching the magazine to my chest, and staring long and hard at her back. (This usually worked when I wanted my mother's attention. It was kind of like a Mexican standoff. She either gave in first, or I just turned around and left her alone.)

This time, though, I had an important question and held my ground. Finally Mom stopped her sewing machine, hitched a small sigh, and asked me what was on my mind.

"I have something really important to ask you," I said as apologetically as I could.

It worked! She turned around and faced me; her sewing put on hold.

"Do you think I can make one of these?" I asked, thrusting the magazine in front of her face.

She jerked back a little, and hesitantly took the magazine from my hand. I believe my mother already knew it would involve a challenge for her, as well as one for me.

What I wanted her to see was under an article headed *"Easy Crafts for Christmas."* It described how to make a coat pin that looked like a small Christmas wreath. The steps were enumerated one by one. She carefully read the instructions, and then looked up at me. "I don't see why you couldn't make one of these. The article describes exactly what to do. If you take your time and follow the directions, I believe you could make one."

"But, Mom, it says to cut out a circle on a piece of stiff cardboard, about three inches around. And then draw a smaller circle, two inches around, in the center of the bigger circle. How do I do that? I can't draw a round circle."

"Well, it's difficult for anyone to draw a perfect circle. You need to use something for a pattern."

"Oh, yeah..." I acknowledged, and then didn't continue my sentence. I stood there looking wide-eyed and stupid.

Mom kind of shook her head slightly, and looked back at the picture in the magazine. "I have an idea," she said. (I knew she would!) Then she started rummaging around in her knick-knack box.

"Ah, I knew I had one in here." She held up a window shade pull ring. (You know what I mean, one of those round plastic rings that hung down at the end of the string used to pull a window shade up and down). It was a perfect circle with a small circle in the center! I swear she was a genius, and she could be relied on every time you needed her help! I loved Mom a lot, but better than that, I deeply respected her. Throughout my life I listened when she spoke to me. Oh, yes, when I got older, I would often argue a point (that's what teenagers are supposed to do), but I *always* listened.

"And, I do believe I have the perfect piece of cardboard for you to use." She rummaged around again, this time in her remnant cabinet. Voila! She pulled out a perfect rectangular piece of cardboard. The kind that was used in hosiery packages to display the nylons. I momentarily stared at her cabinet. It was like a magic place—it was a small, neatly organized cabinet, out of which she could pull anything (sometimes rarely needed items). How did she do that?

"Here (she handed me the piece of cardboard), you can draw your wreath on this."

"Okay, but I gotta draw lots of wreaths."

"Why?"

"'Cause, I'm gonna sell them to make money for Christmas."

"Oh dear," she said softly. "Who are you going to sell them to?"

"Lots of people we know. I need about $3.00 for Christmas, and I thought I could sell them for about 10 cents each."

"Well, that could be a lot of work. Are you sure you want to do this?"

"Yup!"

"Okay, you start by drawing your wreaths. If you need more cardboard, let me know." She turned back to her neglected sewing, and I skipped out of the room, cardboard and shade ring in hand, to find my scissors and a pencil.

* * *

The only desk in the house was Dad's, and kids weren't allowed to use it for coloring or scribbling or any other kid project. So, I chose the dining room table on which to start my Christmas wreaths. I found that using the shade ring was relatively easy and went quickly. I had to return to the sewing room to get two more pieces of cardboard; I could get 9 rings per sheet, allowing enough room between them to get my scissors around each wreath without cutting into the one beside it. Some of the wreaths were not quite perfect; the ring shifted a little while I was tracing it, but they were close enough to pass.

The next step was to cut them out, a task that proved to be harder than I thought it would be. It was relatively easy to cut the wreaths out of the cardboard—I could have used a sharper scissors, but I knew better than to ask Mom for one of her sewing scissors. So, I persevered and got through the first piece of cardboard. (My little scissors left red marks on my thumb and pointer finger from having to use a lot of pressure on the cardboard. I hoped the next step went easier.)

I poked my scissors into the middle of the first wreath. The rounded tips wouldn't go through the cardboard, so I poked harder. It finally went through the center of the wreath and completely through the side as well. It was ruined! Oh, well—it was a good thing I had drawn some extras. I tried the next one. This time the scissors would not punch through the center, no matter how hard I pushed. The little wreath bent in half and would not straighten out again. Another one ruined!

I obviously had the wrong implement for the job. I got up and went into the kitchen to retrieve one of Mom's paring knives. I was exasperated enough to not consider or even care if it would be allowed. The knife definitely had a sharp point.

I returned to my project, armed. The paring knife easily punched through the third wreath, and pierced into my first finger. "*Ouch!*" I cried out, and immediately stuck my finger in my mouth. I looked around, and hoped I hadn't been heard. I wasn't supposed to be using the paring knife. I sat there, finger stinging and eyes watering, wondering what to do next.

About that time Jimmy, my older brother, came down the stairs from his room. "Was that you who hollered?" he asked. "What'cha doin'?"

"Nothin'." I replied, with my finger still stuck in my mouth.

"Let me see your finger," he said, reaching for my hand.

I jerked away. "No, it's none of your business."

"Were you playing with the paring knife?"

"I wasn't playing with it. I was trying to cut out the center of these dumb wreaths, and I stuck myself. It's really bleeding, and hurts!" Defiantly I stuck my finger back in my mouth.

"Get your finger out of your mouth before you get blood poisoning. I'll get you a bandage." He went into the kitchen and got a bandage out of the "junk" drawer. (Mom had bandages stashed in about every room in the house—you never knew where an accident would happen.)

After Jim tended my wound, he turned his attention to my project. He picked up my cutout wreaths, and said for me to follow him up to his room.

Out of his closet, he got an old cutting board Mom had given him to use when he was working on his balsam airplanes. Then he searched through the drawer on his small worktable, and came up with a small box of used razor blades.

"What are you doing with those!" I gasped.

"I use them to cut out my airplanes—that way I get a clean edge."

"Does Mom know you have those?"

"I don't think so, but it doesn't matter. I've been using them long enough to know how to be careful. And, you don't need to snitch on me, that is, if you want me to help you cut out your wreaths."

"I won't," I promised in a small voice.

He set about the task with a serious determination, concentrating on each wreath as though it was a piece of art. When my brother was focused and involved, one did not interrupt him! So, I just stood off to the side and watched. In no time at all he had all the wreaths cut out (including the centers), and I was sent off to accomplish the next step on my own. He did not ask me why I needed all those wreaths—it's like he knew it was another one of my "projects," and it was safer not to know.

* * *

According to the magazine instructions, that next step was to wrap my wreaths with green yarn. To secure the fabric around the wreath, it was necessary to lock the loops of yarn with a chain knot. The easiest way was to use a large darning needle. Oh, yeah, easy for who? I headed back to the sewing room.

"Hey, Mom! You got another minute?"

With a small sigh, Mom said, "Yes, dear, what do you need help with now?"

"What's a chain stitch?"

"Why do you need to know about a chain stitch?"

Once again the magazine was thrust under my mother's nose. She quietly read the next step in the creation of the Christmas wreaths.

"I see," she said. "Now that makes good sense." (I don't know if she was talking to me or to herself.) I stood there silently, looking expectantly at her.

"Did you bring a wreath with you?"

"Yup, I brought all of them."

"I just need *one* to show you how to do this, Donna."

"Oh." I said resignedly. I was not going to get by that little task—Mom was not Jim.

First, she produced a large darning needle from another magical drawer. It had a very large eye, making it easy to thread the yarn through it. She slowly showed me how to start the green yarn on the wreath cutout, by holding the end of the yarn in place while making two wraps around the wreath with the bulk of the yarn. The yarn did not pull loose. Then she showed me how to make a loop with the yarn on the outside edge of the wreath, thread the yarn through the loop, and pull it tight. It made this perfect little knot (a chain stitch) on the outer rim.

"Now, you repeat this step all around the wreath," she told me with encouragement. "Want to try it?"

"Sure," I said confidently. My first attempt did not go as smoothly as Mom's. She made me do it over. The second and third time ended with the same haphazard result.

"What am I doing wrong?" I asked her in frustration.

"You just need to go more slowly, and practice some more. You'll get it. Remember, 'if at first you don't succeed, try and try again.'"

I looked at her with furrowed brows as she turned around and resumed what she was doing before I came into the room. With a sigh, I turned around and went back to the dining room.

Well, I kept at it until bedtime. Mom walked through the room several times, stopping to inspect my work and letting me know when I had to "redo" some of it. I thought they all looked okay, and wished she were less critical. I only got seven done. The next night I moved my manufacturing department upstairs to my bedroom. All in all it took me the rest of the week to finish my project.

After wrapping and chain stitching my wreaths, I had to attach three little red beads on each one for holly berries. Then I sewed a small red bow on the top of each wreath. Mom gave me the narrow, satin ribbon, but I had to make the little bows by hand; another step that didn't go as easily as the directions said they would. Finally Mom helped me attach a small gold safety pin on the back of each wreath to secure it to a lapel or collar. I thought the wreaths had turned out fairly good, in spite of a few flaws here and there.

Nowhere in that article did it say how long it would take or how hard it was to make those little Christmas wreaths. They should have printed a *difficulty rate* from one to ten at the end of each project.

*   *   *

We all attended catechism (kind of like Sunday School for Catholic children) on Saturday mornings. When it was time to leave, I came downstairs carrying the shoebox I stored my "good" shoes in.

"Why do you have your good shoes under your arm?" Mom asked guardedly.

"Oh, these aren't my good shoes. I'm just temporarily borrowing the box for my Christmas wreaths."

"Okay," Mom paused, "then why are you taking your Christmas wreaths to catechism?"

"I thought I could sell a few right after catechism to some of the kids' moms."

"Donna, I'm not sure catechism is the right place to sell your wreaths. That is God's time, not yours."

"I'm not sellin' them *during* catechism! I'm sellin' them *after* catechism! I figured that time was up for grabs to anyone that needed to use it."

"Oh, dear," Mom said more to herself than me. "All right, just don't make a pest of yourself. And put your good shoes back in that box when you get done using it!"

* * *

There was no need for Mom to be concerned about my pestering people after Catechism. Most of the kids' moms were waiting in their cars keeping the heaters running. They weren't standing outside visiting as they usually did. I guess it was a little bit too cold for that. The kids ran out of the parish center, jumped in the cars and their moms took off without looking back. Jim said they probably knew I was going to ambush them, and escaped in the nick of time. (Oh boy, he was a great comedian! I told him he needed to be on the radio!) I did manage to corner two of the catechism teachers; each one bought a wreath. But, I knew this meant a long afternoon for me. I still had lots of wreaths to sell.

After lunch I bundled up and got ready to hit the streets. Mom wished me luck, and told me to be back home around 4:00 p.m.

Now, "selling" was right up my alley. I enjoyed it, and was not overly shy about approaching people to buy my item. In my mind I had laid out my route, and knew which houses I would call on. "Negative perspiration", as Dad would have said.

As things turned out, I ran out of wreaths before calling on all my potential customers. Several people bought more than one! I had little opposition to my product after I explained that I had made the wreaths by myself and by hand. I showed them where I had cut myself with the knife and poked my fingers with the needle. They were more willing to buy after that. Years later I found out that my presentation was referred to as a "sympathy close." Whatever it was called, it worked quite well!

I was quite pleased with myself. The wreath project had been successful, and I had enough money to buy the Christmas gifts I had planned to give to each member of the family. I was also looking forward to seeing my little Christmas wreaths pinned on the coats of women who went to Midnight Mass on Christmas Eve.

* * *

December 24th finally arrived. When we went to Midnight Mass, I made sure I sat at the end of the pew, near the center aisle. That way I could see the women as they passed by, and check if they were wearing their wreaths.

As the church steadily filled with people, I had yet to see any of my wreaths pinned to any of the coats of the women who had bought one (except my mother, that is). I gradually became more concerned. I leaned over to my mother, and whispered, "No one's wearing her wreath. If they didn't want to wear it, why did they buy one?"

"Maybe they are saving it until Christmas Day, Sweetheart."

My mother was trying to reassure me, and save my feelings, but it wasn't working. I looked around the church again, but could not spot any of my wreaths. Then it dawned on me, "They bought the wreaths to be nice, not because they thought the wreaths were pretty!"

For some reason, I felt guilty. I didn't want them to buy the wreaths to be nice. I wanted them to buy them because they liked the wreaths. As I thought more and more about the situation, I became more and more embarrassed. I guess the wreaths were pretty yucky, and I wasn't very good at making craft things. Mom was right. I needed to take more time and do things more slowly.

As I sat there feeling very miserable, I made a decision. Somehow, and I didn't quite know how at that time, I would give them back their money and apologize for the badly made wreaths. It was the only right thing to do! Next year I would sell those boxed Christmas cards instead (even though I thought they were pretty blah).

My mother's whisper interrupted my thoughts, "Donna, look over there at Mrs. Donnelly."

Mass had started, and since people were no longer opening the main doors frequently, it had become warmer in the church. Several women had taken off their coats, including Mrs. Donnelly. On her dress collar, she was wearing the Christmas wreath I had sold to her!

I couldn't help myself—I sat forward and craned my head to both sides and front and back of our pew. I saw little Christmas wreaths pinned to the clothes of several women! They *did* like them! I felt delighted. I had not failed! I just wanted to jump up and yell "Merry Christmas" everyone. But I contained myself, and waited until after mass. Then I hurried outside, with an enormous grin on my face, to wish as many people as I could "Season Greetings."

The next Christmas I by-passed all craft projects. I had learned my limitations when it came to producing hand made items—I just didn't have the knack or the patience. And, you know what, those companies that make those blah Christmas cards also have brightly boxed rolls of Christmas wrapping paper to sell!

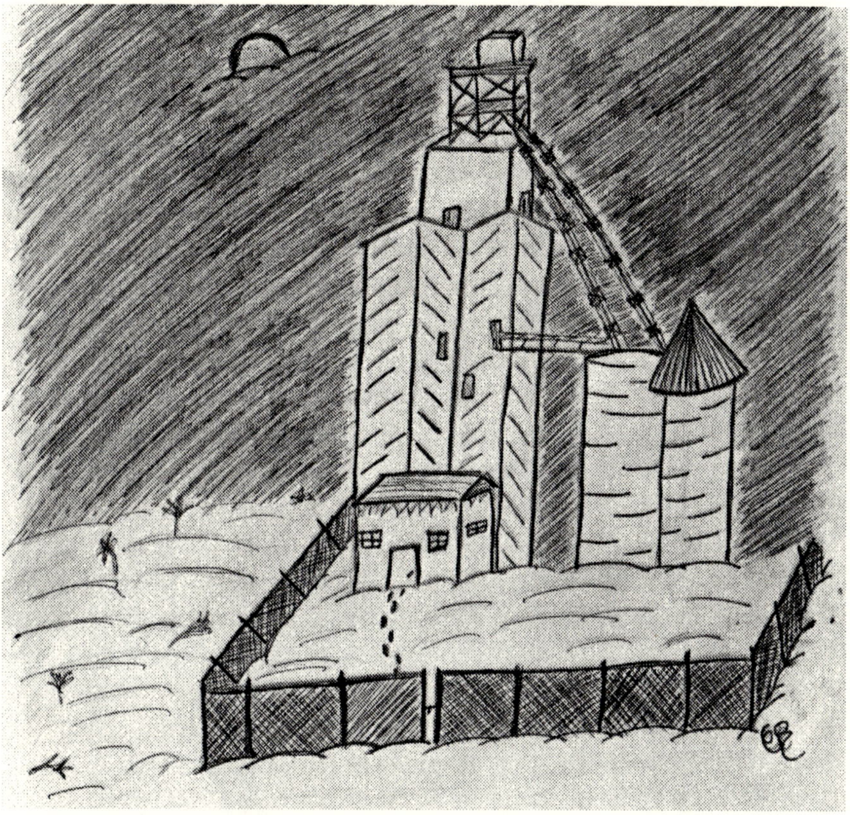

Oh What Fun It Is To Ride In A Four-Door Chevrolet...

...as told by Pat

"Well now, this is interesting." To make sure he had our attention Dad snapped the evening newspaper, glanced around the living room and began to read. "To celebrate this year's Christmas season the town of Parkerville will be featuring the world's tallest Christmas tree. The official lighting ceremony will be held at 6:00 p.m. on Thanksgiving evening, and the tree will be lit and displayed every night from Thanksgiving until Christmas. The Parkerville Boosters Club invites all of their neighbors in nearby towns to come and enjoy this record-breaking display. The merchants of Parkerville will be sponsoring a *Stop and Shop* during this same time period by remaining open until 9:00 p.m. every night except Thanksgiving and Sundays."

He lowered the paper to his lap. "How about that? The tallest Christmas tree in the world right here in Illinois."

My brother Jim sounded very skeptical as he asked, "I bet it's a big tree all right, but how can they be sure it's the tallest one in the whole *world*?"

"Oh, they probably looked it up in one of those world record books, and then made sure they got one a few inches taller. It's a pretty good publicity idea."

"They're probably having it shipped in from northern Minnesota or Wisconsin," added Mom. "I'm sure it'll be very pretty when it's all lit up."

Jim and Donna had been sprawled on the living room floor playing checkers. His interest now aroused, Jim twisted his lanky frame around and sat up. "Gosh, how tall do you think it would have to be to set a new world's record? Fifty or sixty feet?"

"How tall is that?" I asked quickly. At age seven, I still didn't have a firm concept of inches, feet, or yards.

"As tall as a five or six story building, Twerp. Taller than the water tower."

"Wow! A Christmas tree bigger than the water tower? Can we go see it? Can we? Huh? Please…?"

"Oh, well, I don't know. A special trip to Parkerville just to see a tree…"

"Not *just* a tree, Dad," said Donna. "It's a record setting Christmas tree—the tallest one in the world. I think it'd be fun to go and see it."

"Yeah! You want to see it too, don'tcha Jim? Don'tcha? Mom? Do you want to see it? I do! I really, really, really want to go! Can't we?" I turned from person to person, desperately trying to solidify a majority vote for the trip.

"Well, it does sound like something to see. Leonard, how far away is Parkerville?"

"Well, let's see." Dad glanced back at the paper. "Map on page four." He flipped the paper over and studied it for a moment. "Okay, it's a little north of Kankakee, and about 30 miles east of Highway 45. Pretty close to the Indiana line. Nuts! That's a little more than eighty miles one way."

"That's a little far, isn't it? And, of course, to see it lit up we'd have to go at night, or at least come back after dark, on unfamiliar roads…" Mom sounded doubtful, and I could see the trip slipping away. I crossed my fingers, held my breath, and wished for the trip as hard as I could.

"Now wait a minute, Bernice. Let's think about this. They're going to be lighting it for the first time on Thanksgiving, and this year it's our turn to go to Woody and Mary's. We could do Thanksgiving like we always do, but maybe leave Shabanaw a little earlier and stop in Parkerville on the way home. That would only be about thirty miles out of the way."

I let out my breath with a whoosh, but kept my fingers crossed. Now I concentrated on Mom, sending her intense thought waves to "say yes, say yes, say yes…"

"What a good idea, Len. I think that would work out just fine. We'd only need to leave maybe thirty minutes to an hour earlier, and I know Woody and Mary will understand when we explain why. Yes, let's plan on it."

"Yay!" I leapt to my feet and started doing a little Indian dance, complete with chanting, in the middle of the living room. "We're gonna see the Christmas tree, we're gonna see the Christmas tree, we're gonna see…"

"Patty! Calm down. We don't need that kind of rambunctiousness inside the house." Mom glanced at the clock. "Besides, it's time for you to go upstairs and take your bath. Let's get going."

As I bounced out of the living room I heard Dad mutter under his breath, "*What* is the matter with that child?" This was his standard comment about me whenever I did something he thought was odd, and it was always delivered in the tone someone uses when they roll their eyes heavenward and ask, "Why me?" It didn't bother me a bit, because I had other things to think about. I was already trying to envision a Christmas tree taller than the water tower, festooned with lights and sparkling with frost on the branches. It would be a wondrous thing to see.

For me, the rest of the week before Thanksgiving passed in a blur of anticipation. I made a point of telling everyone I knew all about the impending trip to see the world's tallest ever Christmas tree. I drew a picture of a nervous looking turkey next to a pilgrim with an ax, and then presented it to our neighbor Mrs. Nelson, cunningly using the social occasion as an opportunity to tell her all about the tree. I even cornered people whom I didn't know and told them, if I could get them to stand still long enough to hear about it. I carefully counted off each day until Thanksgiving.

* * *

"Donna? Patty? Come on girls, time to get up now." I opened my eyes to a room filled with the faint, mauve-tinged light of pre-dawn. Mom was standing between our beds, alternately shaking our shoulders gently as she tried to rouse us.

"Izz too early," I muttered as I snuggled deeper into my warm little nest.

"No, it's not. Come on now; it's Thanksgiving morning and we have a long trip to make. Let's get up now." I pretended I didn't hear that as I slid back into sleep. I could hear Donna moving around in her bed and yawning. Mom tried again with me, "Okay, Patty, up now." My shoulder was shaken again. "It's Thanksgiving. Of course, if you really don't want to go, I guess we could leave you at home, but then you'd miss seeing the Christmas tree tonight."

A cattle prod could not have had a better effect. My eyes snapped open and I sat up so quickly I made myself dizzy for a moment. How could I have forgotten? *The* Christmas Tree was on the schedule for tonight! "Okay, Mom, I'm up. Let's go!"

"Well, first change out of your pajamas and then come downstairs for breakfast. We'll go as soon as everyone is done eating."

We didn't leave immediately after breakfast. First the dishes and kitchen had to be cleaned up, and then Dad insisted that everyone make "bathroom runs" so that he could avoid unscheduled stops on the way. Finally, bundled up against the cold, we piled into the car and left for Shabanaw. The sun had just lifted above the horizon, and everything sparkled with the night's frost.

We arrived at the Hagen's to find that Woody and Mary had a houseful of friends and relatives gathered to celebrate the holiday. That was fine with me since it gave me a new audience to listen to me carry on about the Christmas tree. I had to compete for time with Woody, who was showing off their brand new television set (a big deal in 1955), but I managed to corner a sizable number of victims, some of them more than once. By 12:30 I had made such a pest of myself that Mom banned me to the outdoors until dinner was ready.

I sat on the top step of the porch, impatiently tapping my feet. The Hagen's old dog, a black Labrador mix named Jack, was lying beside me on the porch enjoying a nap in the sunshine. I reached over to pet him and scratch his ears, saying, "Hey, Jack, do you like Christmas trees? 'Cause we're gonna go see the world's biggest ever Christmas tree tonight. Jim says it'll probably be bigger than the water tower and it'll have lights and ornaments and stuff all over it. Isn't that *cool?*"

Jack lifted his head, thumped his tail on the porch a few times, and swiped me once across my cheek with his wet tongue. Then he lowered his head with a sigh, twitched a little bit in his patch of sunlight, and went back to sleep. All in all, Jack had been more appreciative of the story than most.

Mom finally called me in for dinner, gave me a few dire warnings about what would happen if I didn't stop bothering people, and then turned me loose to enjoy the rest of the day. The day passed as Thanksgiving usually does—a relaxed day of good food, good people, and good feelings and thanks for all that we have. For me, the day carried the extra glow of the promised treat at the end that would also be a spectacular start to the Christmas season.

We left the Hagen's a little before sunset and headed south. As the miles slipped away behind us on U.S. 45 I grew more and more excited. By the time we reached the turn-off for Parkerville it was solidly dark, and Mom was using a small flashlight to read directions from the map that had been in the newspaper. When we first saw the lights of Parkerville, I sat back and closed my eyes—I didn't want to get even a partial glimpse of The Tree, preferring to wait until I heard Mom say "We're here." At that point I would open my eyes and absorb the glory whole. I listened to my mother's soft voice saying, "All right, Len, you go down Main to Pine, then turn left on Pine…now we go to Mill Road and take a right…"

Finally, the car stopped. There was a moment's silence, and then Mom said, "Well, I guess we're here."

Prepared to be awed, I snapped my eyes open and looked around. Nothing. No tree, no lights, not even a scrap of tinsel. I scrambled around so that I was kneeling on the seat, peering out the back window of the car—still nothing. I spun around, checking the view out of each window, hoping that somehow I had missed a 60-foot Christmas tree on first glance, but there was still no tree. "Where is it? Where's the tree?" I wailed. "They said they had a huge tree! What'd they do with it?"

Everyone was looking around in confusion. Mom used the flashlight to check the map again, and then said, "This is where it's supposed to be." She looked around and added, "But this is a strange part of town for Christmas decorations." She was right. We were on the edge of town with windswept cornfields on the other side of the road. Our car was parked next to a tall chain link fence that enclosed a large building with a graveled lot around it, lit by a few yard-lights.

Dad snorted, "Why, this is the damn grain elevator. The paper must have got the map wrong."

When Dad said "grain elevator", Jim rolled down the window on his side of the car and stuck his head out. A moment later he pulled his head back in, and said, "Nope, this is it. Uh, you could probably see it better if we all get out of the car."

Four car doors popped open and we all piled out. I heard Donna start to giggle, but I was still looking around frantically, trying to spot the wondrous tree. Jim tapped me on the shoulder and said, "Um-m, Twerp, the tree is up there." He was pointing to the top of the grain elevator. My gaze followed his arm up to his pointing finger, then jumped to the building and continued up, up, and up to the roof of the grain elevator. There, sporting a few sparkling lights, was the most pathetic excuse for a Christmas tree that I had ever seen in my short life.

My jaw dropped and the air whooshed out of me as I stared at that feeble tree. Then I gulped in a huge breath and started, "But...but...they said...they...that's not...they *said*....*they lied*! They *lied* about the Christmas tree!" My indignation was boundless, and I was on the verge of tears.

"Well, Twerp, sometimes people do that, you know."

I rounded on my brother and shouted, "But it was in the *newspaper*! They *lied* in the *newspaper*! Grown-ups aren't supposed to lie in the newspaper!"

"Sometimes they do that, too, Twerp, but it's usually about politics."

"...or, about UFO's," Mom added quietly.

During this interchange Dad had been standing with his hands on his hips, gazing at the roof of the grain elevator. Now, slowly shaking his head, he turned back to the family. "Jumpin' Jack Jesus, can you believe this shit?"

"Language, Dear, please. And besides," Mom glanced back up at the tree, "I guess you could say that this is the *highest* Christmas tree..."

"Oh, for cripes sake, Bernice. I noticed their directions took us out of the way and made us go all the way down Main Street so we could see all their crummy shops. Look, that's the road back to the highway right over there! C'mon, everybody back in the car. We're going home."

We climbed back in the car, Dad started the engine and, with a chirp of tires and a spray of gravel, we were on our way. We made our way around the grain elevator and, as we pulled onto the blacktop, the tires squealed. We were under way less than a minute when Dad glanced in the rearview mirror and growled, "Now what, for God's sake?" As he slowed down and pulled onto the shoulder we became aware of flashing lights behind us, and something told us these were definitely not Christmas lights.

Jim looked over his shoulder at the car behind us, and said, "It's the fuzz, Dad."

"James! For heaven's sake, it's the police," admonished Mom. As we rolled to a stop she glanced into the back seat and murmured, "All right, kids, let's all just stay calm and *quiet*. We'll be on our way shortly."

Seen from the back seat of our car, the cop who approached Dad's door was just a hulking shadow with an occasional glimmer in the chest area where the cruiser's flashing lights reflected off his badge. We could, however, clearly make out the impressive bulge of a holster at his hip. Dad rolled down his window and hoisted a sickly smile onto his face.

"Good evening, Officer Um-mm, er-r-r, Officer. Can I help you with something?"

"Deputy Doolite. Driver's license."

"Oh, of course." Dad scrambled for his wallet, pulled out his license and handed it over to the cop, who examined it leisurely under the beam of a high intensity flashlight. While the deputy was thus engaged, Dad leaned towards Mom and whispered, "Did he say Deputy Dooright?"

"Doolite, dear, Doo*lite*," Mom murmured back.

The beam of the flashlight then raked across the other occupants of the car.

"Well, Mr. De..., um-mm, DeMuth, I see you're from Paxton. Can I ask what brings you to Parkerville? Visiting family for the holiday, maybe?"

"Actually, we spent the day with friends who live north of here, but we saw the notice in the paper about the Boosters' Christmas tree and thought we'd stop and see it on the way home."
"Uh-huh…"
"Well, that's a really cute publicity idea someone had. How tall is that elevator, anyway?"
"Well, now, we appreciate people visiting our little town, but we'd appreciate it more if they didn't drive so fast when leaving it."
"Was I speeding? I'm sorry, Officer, I didn't realize it. You know, it's been a long day, the family's getting tired, and…"
"I clocked you doing 57 in a 30 mile per hour zone."
"Oh, surely not. I may have been a little over the limit, but…"
"Are you questioning my equipment or my judgment, Mr. DeMuth?"
"Oh, no, no—nothing like that. I don't remember seeing a speed limit sign and it's a rural blacktop, and, well…Listen, Officer, I'm really sorry about this. I'll be much more careful. You say the limit is 30 through here?"

The cop glanced around the area. We were in the middle of the back of nowhere with not another soul within miles, but he saw fit to continue, "Dark night like this, driving too fast. Maybe someone crossing the road or something. Maybe a tractor pulling out of a field. Could have been a really bad accident."

"Well, I did have my high beams on." Dad was starting to sound a little testy.

The cop's right hand moved toward his hip, and the three of us in the back seat flinched, positive that he was going to pull his gun and drill Dad right there for giving him lip. Instead, he pulled a ticket pad from his back pocket. "Well, Mr. DeMuth, this is what I'm going to do. I'll let you go tonight, get your family on home, but I am going to have to write you a ticket. Going 27 miles per hour over the limit is a little much to let go, you know." He flipped open the ticket pad and started writing.

"A ticket?" Dad asked. "All right, Officer, what do I do? Mail that in?"
"Mail? No, sir, you just follow the directions printed on the bottom of the ticket. You'll need to come back up here next Tuesday for a hearing, and take care of it then in person."
"But, I can't do that. I have to work next Tuesday. Listen, if I agree that I was speeding, can't you just tell me what the fine is and let me mail it in.?"
"No, you've got to appear in person. Next Tuesday, 10:00 a.m."

"But, that's impossible." A distinct note of desperation was creeping into Dad's voice. "Look, Officer, isn't there some way we could take care of this tonight? Maybe I could appear before the sheriff or the J.P. or someone?"

"It's Thanksgiving, and it's 8:00 at night."

"Couldn't you try?"

The cop tapped his pen against his teeth for a few seconds, then said, "You stay put, right here, and I'll be back in a minute." He walked back to the cruiser and climbed in.

The second he cleared the rear of our car, our back seat burst out in a good imitation of a tragic Greek chorus.

"It's a holiday. Why does he have to give you a ticket?"

"Can he put Daddy in jail?"

"Will we all have to go to jail?"

"He sure looks mean, doesn't he?"

"Will you kids pipe down! I don't need any comments from the peanut gallery right now!" Dad glanced in the rearview mirror. "Deputy Dooright is coming back. Just give me a break and be quiet!"

"Doo*lite!*" the three of us hissed from the back seat.

The cop was back at Dad's window. "All right, Mr. DeMuth, it's a little irregular but I got hold of the judge, and he's going to make an exception, seeing as how it's a holiday and all."

"Then I can mail in the fine?"

"No, sir, you can follow me back into town, and we'll take care of this tonight."

"Well, all right. Thank you, Deputy Dooright. Lead the way."

As the cop walked away, we rolled our eyes and groaned, "Doolite, Dad, it's Doo*lite!*"

The cop was back at his car again and a few seconds later pulled onto the road with his lights still flashing. As he passed us, Dad pulled in behind him and we made a little parade of two going back to Parkerville. The cop did not turn off the cruiser's lights. We followed him through town and into a small parking lot next to a building.

Mom peered through the windshield and remarked, "Why, I believe this is a tavern. Isn't that odd?"

"Well, Bernice, you're right. It *is* a tavern, but Deputy Dooright over there seems to think it's the right place." Dad tipped his head towards the tavern where the cop was now standing near the door, arms crossed and staring at our car as he patiently waited for his prisoner to say his last farewells. "I'll be back as soon as I can."

As he opened the car door, Mom said softly, "And remember, dear, it's Deputy Doolite."

With a deep sigh, Dad got out of the car and walked over to the cop, who turned on his heel and led the way into the tavern.

A thoughtful silence descended over the car as the minutes ticked by. We waited. Occasionally one of us would flick a hopeful glance at the tavern door, but it remained obdurately shut. Someone sighed; someone else coughed. We waited. Mom's eyes were almost shut, but her lips moved silently. I suspect she was saying the rosary, and she was probably well into the third decade considering the time that had passed. We continued to wait.

Finally, in a small voice Donna ventured, "Do you think they put Daddy in jail?"

Mom sighed. "No, Sweetheart, I don't think they did that."

"Well, where is he, then? What's taking so long?"

"Your father is in that building; you saw him go in. And it hasn't really been that long. We just need to wait patiently."

We settled back to wait some more. The car was getting colder, and my toes were feeling it. I squirmed around a bit, trying to get more comfortable, and Jim patted my knee. "Hang in there, Patty, it can't be much longer," he said quietly. We waited.

At last, after what felt like hours, the tavern door opened and Dad came out, followed closely by the cop. The cop stopped a few feet into the parking lot and lit a cigarette while Dad continued over to our car. He pulled open the driver's door and slid into the front seat.

"Bernice, do you have any money with you?"

"I might have a little. Why?"

"The fine is fifty bucks, and I've only got twenty-seven dollars on me."

"Oh, well, I have the checkbook." Mom reached for her purse.

"I already tried that. They won't take a check. They want cash on the nail. Do you have any money?"

"Well, let me see. Here, hold the flashlight so I can see in my purse." As Dad aimed the flashlight into the top of her purse, Mom began rummaging. "Now where did I put...oh, yes, here's a five, and...I think...in this pocket, maybe...here are some ones, and...my wallet, yes, here's a ten, and...this outside pocket...oh, that darn zipper always sticks...there it goes...let's see, two more ones, and...oh, where else? Oh, yes, the glove box!" She popped open the glove compartment, shoved Dad's maps around, slid her hand way to the back and produced, "Another five! There, Dear, how much is that?"

Dad was sorting and straightening a handful of crumpled bills, counting as he did so. "Okay, that's twenty-four dollars. That'll cover it."

Mom reached over and plucked a one dollar bill out of the stash and tucked it in her pocket saying, "Actually, since you have twenty-seven you only *need* twenty-three, right? Go pay them and, Leonard?"

Dad was already sliding out of the car but turned back, "Yeah? What?"

"Since it's cash, be sure to get a receipt, all right?"

With a snort of disbelief, Dad slammed the car door and strode back to the tavern. The cop followed him back into the building.

A few minutes later Dad re-emerged from the tavern, and this time he was not followed by any uniforms, a hopeful sign. He strode across the parking lot, got in the car and, without a word spoken, started the engine. Once again the back seat erupted with questions.

"What happened in there, Dad?"

"How come you had to go to the tavern?"

"Is the jail in there?"

"Why'd they want so much money?"

"Give me a minute, kids. Let's just get out of here for now." He backed out of his parking place, changed gears, and eased back across the parking lot. At the street he came to a full stop, flicked on his turn signal, and carefully looked both ways before circumspectly pulling out onto the pavement. We passed through Parkerville at a sedate twenty miles per hour.

"Leonard? What did happen in there?"

"Well, when Deputy Dooright radioed in, someone apparently knew that the J.P. was at the tavern, so they called him and he agreed to "hear the case" tonight. We get in there and he's sitting at the bar, and this guy is half lit already. First thing he does is offer to buy me a drink."

"Oh, goodness! What did you say, Dear?"

"I told him I was tired and still had 80 miles to drive, thanked him, but told him I thought I would do better *without* a drink. So then he makes the barkeep make a pot of coffee, and gets me a cup of coffee, instead. Then he had to figure out where to set up his "bench" for the hearing. We ended up at a table in the back of the bar, him sitting behind it and using a beer bottle as a gavel, and I had to stand in front of the table."

"What happened then?"

"Well, Deputy Dooright…"

"Doolite, Dear."

"Yeah, him. Anyway, he went through his spiel again about speeding and tractors pulling out of fields, and then I got a safety lecture from the J.P. Finally, he bangs the table with the beer bottle and tells me it's a fifty-dollar fine, and they don't take out-of-town checks. Lucky we had the cash. I paid him, wished him a Merry Christmas, and left. Oh, yeah, here..." Dad dug in his pocket and produced a crumpled paper napkin that he handed to Mom. "Here's your receipt."

"Dad, you should have told him farmers are too smart to be driving their tractors around at night," said Donna.

"Or pointed out you've never had an accident," added Jim.

I threw in with, "You *should* have told him it's a rotten Christmas tree, and they shouldn't tell lies in the paper."

"Now hush, you three. Your dad handled it just the way he should have."

By then we had reached the edge of town and Dad made a right hand turn onto the blacktop leading back to the highway. Suddenly, Jim spoke up again, "Dad! You should have..."

Mom quickly interrupted him. "Jim, it doesn't matter now. It's all over, and should-have's and would-have's can't change anything."

"But, Mom, he should have..."

"*Not now, Jim.*"

"Okay. It's cool." Jim settled back into his seat and gazed out the window at the night flowing past.

Dad kept the speedometer nailed to twenty-seven miles per hour until the lights of Parkerville faded behind us. Then, he floored it. As we rolled along, Dad started muttering, obviously replaying the evening in his head. "God forsaken town...stupid Christmas tree...Deputy Dooright...keystone cops and a kangaroo court...*Fifty* dollars, for God's sake...speed trap...lure you in with a lie about their damn tree...*I've* put up better looking trees...ambushing people...*fifty*...maybe they'll make enough money off their speed trap to afford a *real* town tree next year..."

The night had been emotionally draining, leaving all of us tired and longing for the lights of home. The heater was again pushing out a cozy flow of warm air, and Dad's muttering was almost like listening to droning bees. My head slumped against Donna's shoulder as I dozed off.

I don't know how long I slept, but the next thing I was aware of was Dad's voice. "Cripes, look at that. We're going to have to stop for gas."

"Len, do you think we'll find a station open this late on Thanksgiving?"

"Oh, yeah. Once we hit Route 45 there'll be something."

"How much further to 45, Dear? It seems like we should have crossed it by now."

"Just a little further. It's gotta be just a few miles. Um-m-m-m, Bernice, I know you have a dollar, but do you have any other cash tucked away somewhere? I'm gonna need at least a couple of dollars for gas to get us home."

"I'm sorry, Dear, that dollar is all I have left. Do you think someone would take a check?"

"Not an out-of-town one, not for gas. Hey, kids! Do you guys have any money? I need to borrow it for gas, but I'll pay you back when we get home. I'll go to the bank tomorrow."

Jim dug in his pocket, and I heard the jingle of change. "Yeah, Dad, I've got $1.75 you can have."

Donna was also counting coins. "I've got $1.44. Some of my paper route people paid me yesterday 'cause they were going out of town."

"I have 96 cents," I piped up.

"What? Where?" Dad asked.

"In my marble bag at home. I'm gonna use it to get Christmas gifts."

"In your marble bag? Now, how the hell is that going to be any help..."

"Now, Leonard, you only asked if they had money. You didn't ask how much money they had *with* them."

Before an argument could erupt, Jim interrupted, "Hey, Dad, that sign back there said Indianapolis, but I couldn't read how far. We went by it too fast."

"What? What sign? I didn't see any sign." Dad glanced at the gas gauge again and added, "The only signs you kids need to be looking for are gas station signs. If everyone keeps an eye out, we ought to be able to spot one."

We drove on through the night, but now the three of us had a game to play. Who would be first to spot a gas station sign? About 10 minutes later, Jim won the game. "Dad, there's a Shell sign up there, and it's lit up." Sure enough, that beautiful golden shell was glowing against the sky, and now the scattered lights of a small town began to show up in the same area. A few minutes later, we pulled into the gas station.

In typical 1950's style, the attendant hustled out to our car to see how he could help us. Dad ordered $4.19 worth of gas and, for that, the gas was pumped, the oil and water checked, and both the windshield and headlights were washed and polished. It was all done without one of us setting foot outside of the car.

When the attendant came to Dad's window to collect the money, Dad handed him a wrinkled dollar bill and a fistful of change that included a lot of pennies. The man took the money without complaint, and carefully counted it out. When he had finished, Dad casually asked him, "So, how far to Kankakee?"

"Kankakee? In Illinois?"

"Yeah, Kankakee. Or, how far to U.S. 45?"

"Well, both Kankakee and 45 are about 50 miles or so back the way you just came from."

"Really? Where are we, then?"

"Why, you're in Indiana." The man added the name of the town, but that has been long lost in the mists of memory. What we all heard clearly, however, was that we weren't even in the right state.

Dad dredged up a smile from somewhere and said, "Thank you very much. You've been most helpful. Happy Thanksgiving."

"You're welcome, sir, and a Happy Thanksgiving to you and your family."

Dad pulled away from the pumps, made a U-turn onto the blacktop, and we were off again. "Now, how the hell did we end up in Indiana?"

"That's what I was trying to tell you, Dad, back when we left Parkerville," said Jim. "I was trying to tell you that you should have turned *left* instead of right."

There was a moment's silence and then Mom said, "I'm sorry, Jim, I interrupted you and cut you off. That was rude of me. If I had let you talk we would have saved a lot of time and headache. But, we're headed the right way now, and we'll be home soon."

The rest of the trip passed without incident, and we finally arrived at home about three hours later. Mom had to wake up the three of us to get us into the house and up to our bedrooms.

Donna and I were in our pajamas and ready to turn off the light when Jim tapped on our doorframe. "Hey, girls, can I come in for a minute?"

"Sure. Come on."

Jim came in and sat down on my bed beside me. "Okay, Twerp, listen up. Now, don't bother Dad about this tomorrow, but Paxton is putting up *their* Christmas tree tomorrow. You know, up on Main Street? And it may not be the biggest tree in the world, but it's always pretty big and it sure is pretty. We'll figure out a way to go see it, okay?"

"Okay! When do you think we can go?"

"We'll talk about it tomorrow. Maybe we can go on Saturday and watch the Christmas parade, then check out the tree afterwards. You go to sleep now." With that Jim went back to his room and we turned out the lights. I fell asleep quickly, and spent the night dreaming of a *real* town Christmas tree.

'Tis the Season

...as told by Donna

Mom had the flu, Jim had the flu, and Pat had the flu. Everyone in our house had the flu except me—and it was the Saturday after Thanksgiving! Santa Claus was coming to town! This was not just an important event of the year; it was *the* event of the year! I didn't want to miss it; no, I couldn't miss it. I had waited all year for this day, and, by golly, I was going to see Santa.

Santa either rode into town on a sleigh (if it had snowed recently and there was a decent amount of snow left on the ground), or on a brightly decorated hay wagon (if there was no snow). At the far north end of Main Street was the town Christmas tree, towering anywhere from 18 to 20 feet high, all aglitter with lights and spectacular ornaments. Santa would start his trip from the south end of Main (about eight blocks away from the tree) and slowly ride the length between these two points, waving at all the residents lined up along the street. He greeted the populace with a great many "Ho-Ho-Ho's" and "Merry Christmas's." His jovial arrival meant that Christmas had officially begun.

I wasn't quite sure I believed in Santa Claus. There were too many questionable particulars about the guy that didn't add up, like flying in a sleigh and coming down chimneys, etc. But on that day my doubts were put aside and I was a true fan. Besides, Santa would hand out bags of candy to each child and listen attentively to each request for a fiercely desired Christmas gift. This year I was going to go all the way and ask for a new bike! I pined (no seasonal pun intended) for an *English racer* with sleek narrow wheels that would allow the rider to travel at the speed of light. Whether or not Santa was real didn't matter. What mattered was that I used all my options to get that new bike.

At breakfast that morning Mom had said that, if she felt better by noon, she would drive me downtown. If she wasn't better, I'd have to skip seeing

Santa for that year. That was not good enough for me. It looked as though I had a less than a fifty-fifty chance of seeing Santa, and I needed to change those odds in my favor before eleven o'clock in the morning. Santa was appearing at one p.m. and if I was going to have to walk downtown, I needed to leave no later than eleven. Mom would just have to let me go, and I needed to convince her it would be all right.

I went downstairs and softly knocked on my mother's bedroom door. I held my breath until I heard her hoarsely say to come in. I hoped she had already been awake and just resting instead of me waking her up. I crossed my fingers behind my back and entered her bedroom.

"Are you feeling any better?" I asked.

"Oh, sweetheart, I know you want to go and see Santa, but there is no way I can take you downtown. I'm running a temperature and feel very weak. Please understand."

"It's really okay, Mom," I said, "and I know you need to get well, but I wanted to ask you a favor."

"What is that, dear?"

I started my argument, "Well, you know how you're always telling me that I act like such a big girl, and do my chores and things pretty good, and that no one would guess I was just seven years old because I'm so responsible."

"Yes, you are very responsible, and I've said that many times."

"Well," I started again. "I know the way downtown and back home,…and there's no snow on the ground to get a person cold and wet,…and I would dress very warm,…and watch out for traffic,…and come right back home…that is, if you would let me walk downtown and see Santa. I'd be really okay, and then you could stay in bed and get better. What do you think?" (I squeezed my crossed fingers together as hard as I could.)

"I know there's no snow on the ground, but it's still very cold out there. I don't want you to get this flu too," Mom said in concern. "Maybe your Dad will be back before one o'clock and he can take you downtown."

"Oh no, Mom, you know he never gets home that early when he works on Saturday. I can't count on that!" I pleaded, "Please, please, please let me walk downtown. I promise I'll dress very warmly, and I won't dawdle. I'll see Santa, and come right back home."

Mom didn't say anything for a minute or two. She just looked at me with a great deal of sympathy and then sighed in resignation. "Are you sure you want to walk all the way downtown and back? Donna, it is extremely cold out there". (I just nodded my head "yes") She paused, and then continued, "I want you to wear your heavy coat with a sweater under it, your leggings, a scarf *and* a hat, and your mittens. Agreed?"

She was saying okay! I could hardly believe my ears! I spewed out all my promises again and readily agreed with her wishes. She was the greatest Mom in the world, and I was the luckiest daughter on earth! I sprang to her bedside and gave her a big hug. "Thank you, thank you, thank you!" I cried. "I'll ask Santa to bring you something really nice."

"Don't worry about asking for anything for me. But I do want you to ask him for two bags of candy that you can take home for your sick brother and sister. Okay?"

"I will. I promise I will." And with that said, I sprinted out of her room and headed upstairs to choose what I would wear. Mom called after me to come and see her before I left. I said I would, and that she could even inspect what I had on. Boy, this was going to be a glorious day after all!

I first put on a thermal undershirt and leggings, then my favorite red wool sweater, my snow pants (even though there wasn't any snow), and wrapped a scarf around my neck several times. I carried my snow jacket, mittens, hat and earmuffs that I would put on right before I left the house. The only items I cheated on were my shoes. I had put on two pairs of socks and then my Sunday shoes. I figured Mom wouldn't be able to see my feet when I went into her bedroom to say good-bye. I did not want to wear my school shoes, which I believed were too practical for such an occasion, and my play shoes were just plain ugly. Besides, the streets were dry and I would be careful not to get them dirty.

I was excited! I tried to patiently wait until eleven o'clock, but it wasn't easy. The only thing that kept me in check was a slight modesty; I didn't want to arrive too early and look too greedy to the town folks who would be crowding the downtown starting their Christmas shopping. Finally the time arrived to tell Mom I was leaving.

She gave me a quick, but thorough, look-over, and then told me to have a good time and be careful. Just as I had thought, she didn't see my shoes, and I skipped out of the house feeling confident in my appearance.

Mom was right. It was *very cold* outside. By the time I had gotten to the end of our lane my cheeks were rosy, my nose was red and my toes felt frozen. I walked as fast as I could, trying to keep warm, and kept myself going by practicing my request to Santa in my mind. About half way down town, I had a moment of weakness and wondered if I should turn around and go back home to thaw. But the thought passed quickly and I continued my journey—there was too much at stake for me to wimp out.

I loved downtown at Christmas time. The very practical commercial area of our town was transformed into a once-a-year magical place. All the stores and light posts and parking meters were adorned with colorful seasonal decorations. There were strings of Christmas lights strung from the second stories of the buildings back and forth across Main Street. The store clerks and the patrons were in high spirits wishing everyone a very merry Christmas. All the farmers from around the area would come to town, and, while their wives and kids were shopping, they would stand around outside of the stores in little groups, talking and laughing and swapping stories. On the Saturday when Santa came to town there was an extra amount of anticipation added to all this holiday spirit. I didn't know who invented Christmas, but it was a grand idea!

I slowly walked down the length of Main Street, looking in the store windows and staying out of the way of the busy shoppers. I couldn't help it, but I had a big smile on my face. Everyone in town knew just about everyone else. So, as I went along the streets, I was greeted merrily and warmly. I passed Mrs. Nelson and she stopped me to inquire about where my brother and sister were. I told her that they had the flu, and that Mom was sick too. She said she would bring something by our house later that day for Mom so that she wouldn't have to get up and cook dinner for us. I told her that would be really neat and Mom would appreciate it. She patted me on the head, wished me "Merry Christmas" and went on her way.

The parade started exactly at one p.m. as scheduled. It was not an extremely large parade, but eventful enough to announce the arrival of Santa Claus. The Chamber of Commerce representatives were the first in line in the parade. They carried a large banner that said "Merry Christmas" on it, and waved at everyone as they went by. Next came the women from the Wives Auxiliary, all dressed up like Mrs. Santa Claus. I waved at them as they passed, and giggled to myself. *I didn't know Santa Claus had six wives!*

This was followed by the high school band, with a high-stepping majorette in front. The V.F.W. provided a color guard, and they were followed by the girl scouts and the boy scouts.

In the middle of the parade was the hay wagon with Santa. He was sitting up on a red throne with fake snow covering the platform under his feet. Posted at the corners of the wagon were four large candy canes with huge red bows tied around them. There was a small sign on a post to the left of Santa's chair that said "North Pole," and placed just to his right was an enormous red sack filled with small bags of candy.

Dancing and skipping around Santa's wagon were people dressed like elves. They looked really silly because they were grown-ups dressed in tights and elf gear. I had to laugh out loud when I saw Mr. Archer from our church. He was tall and really skinny, and his green tights made his legs look too long for any human's body. Directly following Santa was the Methodist choir who were singing Christmas songs to scratchy music coming from a recorder placed in the back of the wagon. It was all really quite wonderful, and I couldn't help but clap and wave as they went by. The freezing walk downtown had been worth every step.

After the parade had passed, I started to make my way down to the north end of town. Santa would stop the wagon right next to the big Christmas tree; his helpers would lower the back board, and then place wooden steps up against the side. The kids from town lined up before the first step, and waited until Santa gave the sign for the first one to come up and see him. I was about three-quarters of the way back in the line. It was still quite cold, but I patiently waited, dancing around a little in place to keep warm. One by one we advanced closer to that first step leading up to Santa's lap.

At last, I was the third one back in line. There were two brothers in front of me, and then it would be my turn. I was becoming impatient. To distract myself, I stopped thinking about Santa and took the time to look around once again at the other people milling about the downtown. Just a couple of feet from me were three farmers lounging by a parking meter, talking and laughing about *farmer things*. I noticed that one of the men was occasionally coughing and sniffling. I wondered if he had the same flu that Mom had.

The first of the brothers had gone up the steps and was climbing up onto Santa's lap. I stepped forward and took the position of second in line. With that step, I had also come closer to the group of three farmers. I overheard one of them predicting snow for the beginning of the week. I thought that it would really be nice to have snow for Christmas. Just as that thought came and went, the farmer with the flu let out a huge sneeze. (What followed next was completely astonishing and surreal.) He shook his head back and forth a little, and then reached up to his nose with his right hand. He vigorously blew his nose between his thumb and pointer finger, and, with a practiced flick of his wrist, tossed the *matter* he was holding into the air. The *wad* flipped up and then came down with incredible speed. *Splot!* It landed—dead center on the toe of my right shoe!

I stared at my foot in horror. It was on my shoe! It was a huge mountain of *yuck*, all yellow and globby! I had the most incredible urge to just start screaming and never stop. I looked up at the farmer in disbelief. Unaware of my plight, he was again actively engaged in his conversation with the other two men. How could he be blind to his action? He had just devastated me, and was totally ignorant of it! In panic, I swung my head back and forth, looking around me for help. To my confusion the world was starting to turn gray and blurry, and objects had flickering red auras. I didn't know it at the time, but I was on the verge of fainting. Now frightened, I gasped in great gulps of air. Thanks to my young brain, the chilled air, and the blast of oxygen hitting my system, I managed to control the impending disaster and bring the world back into focus.

I steeled myself and glanced down at my shoe again. I stomped my foot as hard as I could without bringing attention to myself. Oh my God, it was still there, and, I believed, still moving. It was glued to my shoe! I bit my bottom lip to keep my silence. I took a quick inventory of my attire. In all that clothes planning I had not included a handkerchief. I looked frantically over the ground around me. There wasn't even a scrap of paper I could use to wipe my shoe clean. The second brother standing in front of me started up the steps to see Santa. I wanted to yell "Stop! Come back! I'm not ready!" No words came out of my mouth.

Then the clearest thought, final and absolute, came into my mind. I knew without a doubt that I could not ascend those steps and sit on Santa's lap with that *thing* on my shoe. The situation was beyond humiliation—it had graduated to complete horror. I slowly turned, and left my place in line. I swear I heard a funeral dirge playing in the background.

I was not aware of my walk back home. With each step I took, the whirlpool of emotions I felt grew in intensity. I was mad. I was immensely disappointed. I felt betrayed. And, the new attachment to my good Sunday shoe stayed with me all the way. Why? Why had this happened to me on such an important day? What had I done to deserve such a horrible thing? It wasn't fair!

As I started down the lane to our house, the churning inside my chest began to erupt like some enormous, destructive volcano. I stopped mid-way in the road, and the scream I had so maturely controlled spewed from my throat. All my energy flew out with that scream and I plopped to the ground, being careful to keep my fouled shoe separated from any other part of me. I sat there, sobbing and sobbing. I thought it was over, but it wasn't. After the last hiccough of grief, I again felt the irrational nature of the incident. I stood up and started running as fast as I could to reach our back door. Believe it or not, that *alien goo* continued to cling to my shoe. It appeared to have bonded to the leather, frozen there permanently. I could not detach it from either my shoe or my horror!

I flung the door open with a crash and without a break in momentum hit the steps leading up to the inside. Before I could reach the top step, the door opened and my Mother was there, reaching her arms out to me. I slumped against her breast, babbling like a maniac.

"Calm down, Donna. I can't understand a word you're saying. What has happened to you?" Mom asked, extremely concerned.

Without releasing my Mother's protective embrace, I told her the whole ugly story as best I could. It was an exceptional effort to keep my hysteria in check, but little by little, as the words were transferred from my broken spirit to my Mother's concern, I calmed down.

Mom helped me to one of the dining room chairs, and sat me down. Without saying a word, she knelt on one knee in front of me and removed the offensive shoe. She took off the other shoe, stood up and said, "I think a nice hot cup of tea with milk and sugar would be a help, don't you?" I nodded my head "yes."

From the kitchen, Mom's voice said, "Your Dad called ten minutes ago and said he would be home in about thirty minutes. I need a few things from the store, and he agreed to go downtown and pick them up for me. I think you should go with him. I don't know why he couldn't stop by the dime store too, and you could pick out some Christmas candy for you and your brother and sister. There are days when something sweet helps everyone." She walked into the dining room, handed me my cup of hot tea, and gently smiled.

"While we're waiting for your Dad, why don't you and I write a letter to Santa that you can mail when you are downtown?" she suggested. "There's still plenty of time before Christmas, and the Post Office does special deliveries to the North Pole so Santa receives all of the children's letters on time."

"That's a great idea!" I exclaimed. "I can tell him what I want for Christmas, and what Patty and Jimmy want, and how to get to our house…"

"You certainly can, Sweetheart," she interrupted, smiling broadly at my enthusiasm. "We will write a perfect letter to Santa."

After Mom got some paper and a pencil, I stripped off my jacket and scarf, and began composing my letter.

Dear Santa,

You won't believe what happened to me today…

It was going to be a good Christmas after all!

Oh yes, I almost forgot. I did learn something else that day. Wearing your Sunday shoes when you are not supposed to will always bring a certain amount of bad karma. It's a cosmic law.

Christmas Is Coming, One Of the Kids Is Getting Fat?

...as told by Pat

Finding the bags of nuts was a complete accident. It was the weekend following Thanksgiving and the weather, cold and dreary with sleet, discouraged playing outdoors. To keep myself busy, I had decided to "inventory" the shelves and cupboards in Mom's sewing room.

I had already sorted the spools of thread, arranging them in their drawer in prismatic order. Mom didn't require that of me—I did it simply because I thought it looked neat. Also, it pleased me to think that the next time Mom opened that drawer she would be greeted with a rainbow. Now, I was going through the cabinet where material was stored, carefully refolding pieces that had become mussed and trying to guess what type of garments Mom had in mind for the different colors and textures of fabric. I had finished with the top shelf and proceeded to the second one when I noticed that the stacked fabric appeared lumpy.

I reached out with my hand and carefully pressed down on the top of the fabric. It crackled in response. I pressed again—more crackling. My curiosity was immediately fired; crackling was not a natural sound for fabric! I cautiously slipped my hand down behind the cloth, feeling my way downward until my fingers touched something crisp and slick. I ran my fingertips back and forth on this surface and the answer came to me—cellophane! I pulled my hand back out, lifted the pile of fabric out of the way, and gazed at my find. I had stumbled across Mom's stash of Christmas nuts!

I sat back on my heels and, using a very critical eye, assessed the four shelves in the cabinet. Yep, no doubt about it—the two middle shelves were showing an unusual amount of lumps and bumps in the material stored there. I let my fingers do some more probing and quickly uncovered bag after bag of nuts. I felt as if I had discovered a trove of pirate gold.

There was reason for my excitement. As children, the only time of the year that we got fresh nuts was Christmas, and the supply only lasted a day or two. I have always loved fresh nuts, and looked forward to getting them each year with great anticipation. It added to the mystique of Christmas, and the "treat" status of the nuts made them taste even better. By finding the hidden nuts, I *knew in advance* that there would be no shortage this year—if I could just be patient until Christmas I was assured of being able to sate my appetite.

I began putting the bags of nuts and the fabric back into the sewing cabinet. Of course, I noted what this year's selection of nuts was going to be as I put them back. There were several bags of mixed nuts consisting of a fairly standard assortment of Brazil nuts, walnuts, almonds, and filberts. There were two bags of pecans; nuts that always seemed like naturally packaged Southern sunshine in the middle of a cold Illinois winter. Last, there were the "extra" bags of the family favorites—two additional bags of filberts, and four additional bags of walnuts. On Christmas morning these would be emptied into a huge wooden bowl on the coffee table with nutcrackers and picks close at hand, open for everyone to help themselves. I surveyed the shelves to make sure they looked undisturbed, then closed the cabinet and went in search of something else to do.

The bags of nuts haunted me over the next few days. I would be in the middle of doing my homework, and find that I was doodling little pictures of nuts in the margins of my paper. When I was in the kitchen doing dishes, I was suddenly overcome by a compulsion to pull out the silverware drawer and check that the nutcrackers and picks were still in their place at the very back. Since we were lighting only the first candle in the Advent wreath, I knew it was still a long time until Christmas. I spent a lot of time staring at the calendar, counting the number of days until December 25th.

Next, I began worrying about the security of the nuts. What if someone broke into the house and stole them? Mom would never know until Christmas morning, and then it would be too late! I began doing a nut patrol, making sure I had the opportunity at least twice a day to open the sewing cabinet and check that the nuts were still present and accounted for. Reassured that the nuts were not going anywhere, I had an attack of quality control consciousness—what if the nuts were wormy or mildewed? That would be another Christmas morning disaster, but how could I assure that the nuts were good?

One week after discovering the nuts I was back in front of the sewing cabinet with one of the bags of walnuts in my hands. I was turning it from side to side and peering through the cellophane at the nuts, trying to spot worm holes or any sign of mold. As I turned the bag over once more, the seal at the top caught my eye. The bag had been crimped and heat-sealed, producing a sealed strip about half an inch deep with tiny pleats across the width. The center part of the sealed strip looked a little odd and different. Examining it closely, I discovered that the seal was incomplete—the center was beginning to pull apart. Grasping the two sides of the bag just beneath this fault, I tugged very gently. Another pleat or two let go. A second, cautious tug and the hole enlarged again. I could now get my index finger into the bag and actually touch the nuts. After a little more judicious tugging, the hole was large enough for the nuts to pass through it.

I sat on the floor of the sewing room with the partially opened bag of nuts in my lap, and confronted the terrible demon of temptation. It was still three weeks until Christmas, and these were the *Christmas* nuts.

"Yes, yes," whispered a little voice in my head, "but no one will miss one or two of them."

My conscience chimed in with, "Oh, yes they will. Those nuts are for everybody on Christmas. You're already going to have to explain the hole in the bag. Stop while you're ahead. Put them away!"

My hand trembled over the bag for another second or two, then I picked it up and shoved it back into the sewing cabinet, pushing it down behind the fabric without any thought to appearances. I slammed the doors on the cabinet shut, and ran from the sewing room.

That evening at dinner, Dad lit the second candle in the Advent wreath. Now there were two burning, and two more to go before Christmas, which meant it was still three weeks away. It seemed a long time to wait.

After I went to bed that night, I found myself tossing and turning and unable to sleep, while pictures of that hole in the nut bag ran through my mind. I heard Jim turn off his light and go to bed in the next room. A little later, the television was turned off downstairs, and I heard Dad fussing around in the kitchen getting the coffeepot ready to start first thing in the morning. Shortly after that, he and Mom also went to bed. Silence gradually descended over the house as the family fell asleep, but I was still wakeful.

It was about 11:30 when I could stand it no longer. I eased out of bed, slipped into my warm, fuzzy robe and slid my feet into my slippers. Icy light from a full moon streamed through the window and painted pearly highlights on everything in the room—I could see as well as a cat on the prowl. I tiptoed past my sister's bed, let myself into the upstairs hallway, and silently descended the stairs. I remembered to step close to the wall on the fifth tread so it wouldn't creak, and when I got to the bottom of the stairs I paused, every sense alerted to detect whether anyone had heard me. All I heard was the muffled rumble of Dad's snores. Safe!

I moved through the dining room and kitchen as silently as a wisp of fog, stopping in the kitchen just long enough to ease open the silverware drawer and collect a nutcracker and a nut pick. I slipped these implements into the pocket of my robe, and in seconds I was standing in front of the sewing cabinet.

Mom's sewing room had originally been the back porch of the house. Dad had closed it in to make an extra room that was used for storage and Mom's sewing. This room did not benefit from the central heating in the house. The room faced west, and the entire top half of the western wall was an expanse of double paned glass window. During the day, this acted like a greenhouse and kept the room usable in the winter. During the middle of a bitter winter night, however, the window was covered with frost and the room was like a walk-in cooler. Shivering, I opened the sewing cabinet, pulled my robe tighter around me, and sank down to sit on the very chilly floor.

I pulled out the bag of nuts and squeezed a half dozen walnuts through the hole in the top of it. The nutcracker magically appeared in my hand, and the next thing I knew the first walnut lay in my lap, opened into two neat halves. I grabbed the pick and pried out the rich, plump nut meats which I popped into my mouth before that nagging voice of my conscience could stop me. They were wonderful! I chewed slowly and carefully, savoring the taste. In a matter of minutes the six walnuts were reduced to empty shells lying in my lap.

What should I do with the shells? If I put them in the trash, someone might notice them. Also, when I picked up the bag with the remaining nuts, it appeared to be obviously lacking some volume. I pondered the problem, waiting for inspiration that didn't come. It was late, I was tired and feeling very guilty, and on top of that I was chilled to the bone. Five of the walnuts had cracked neatly in half. One had shattered into several small, jagged pieces. Without thinking, I slipped the ten shell halves back through the hole into the bag. Then I gathered up the pieces of the remaining one, got up from the floor, and went into the kitchen where I pushed the incriminating evidence deep into the trash bag. Satisfied that my crime was temporarily hidden, I slipped back upstairs to bed.

I spent the next day in an agony of suspense, waiting for the plundered nuts to be discovered. Apparently, the other members of my family did not suffer from "nut obsession" as severely as I did—no one noticed. I was shocked. I had raided the Christmas nuts and gotten away with it!

Like other criminals before me, the undiscovered crime gave me a false sense of security. After all, if it was that easy, why not do it again? I had even thought up a way to conceal the evidence. Late that night, I was once again in the sewing room. This time, I came armed with a nutcracker, a pick, a dinner knife, my empty marble bag, and a small bottle of glue.

Slipping several more walnuts out of the open bag, I set to work. Using the nutcracker, I applied gentle pressure along the seam of a walnut. When it began to open, I eased the tip of the dinner knife into the crack, then gently and carefully pried the nut open along the seam. The pick came into play to dig out all the yummy nutmeat without further damage to the shell. I lost a shell or two, but most of them opened like the halves of a clam. It took the patience of Job and the manual dexterity of a safecracker. By the time I was sated, more than half the bag of nuts had fallen prey to my lust.

I had kept the empty nutshells together in pairs, and had also matched up the five from my previous binge. Now I proceeded to glue them back together, giving the appearance of whole, complete nuts. The reconstructed fakes were slipped into my marble bag, and then both bags were tucked back behind the fabric. The few irreparably damaged shells were buried deep in the trash bag.

I have heard that successful crime can be addictive. I can vouch for that statement, because during the next two and a half weeks I made repeated late night visits to the sewing room. When I had emptied the first bag of nuts, I refilled it with the empty, glued together shells. Then I turned on Mom's iron, which was always conveniently left on the ironing board in the rear of the sewing room. With the iron set on "low", I painstakingly fitted the top of the nut bag back together and resealed it with a light pressing. Foolproof! It was like a "locked door" mystery. If the bags were still sealed, the crime would be blamed on some ravenous employee of the nut company.

By the 22nd of December, the four extra bags of walnuts were all filled with fakes. The other nuts had been spared, but not through any mercy of mine—I had examined them and found that, unfortunately, Mother Nature had not provided them with a handy seam. I decided that I could wait until Christmas for the filberts, almonds and pecans.

Christmas Eve finally arrived. The gifts to and from members of the family were under the Christmas tree, and Mom had the radio tuned to a station playing carols. The "Santa" gifts would be added after Midnight Mass when the children were asleep—my little brother was still young enough to believe in Santa Claus. We each got to open one gift before we left for Midnight Mass. Mine was a new slip from my godmother. Oh well, morning was not that far away.

After Midnight Mass, we returned home and it was now *officially* Christmas. My little brother was sound asleep on Mom's shoulder when she carried him in from the car. While she took care of putting Raymond in his jammies, Dad hustled Donna, Jim and me off to bed. It was one night of the year when we cooperated admirably, knowing that we would probably be up again by 6:00 or 7:00 in the morning.

I lay in bed and listened to the sounds drifting up from the downstairs. Mom and Dad were busy putting the final touches on Christmas: Santa gifts were brought out of hiding and placed under the tree, baby Jesus was placed into the manger in the crèche, plates of Christmas cookies and fruitcake were set out, and the bags of candy and nuts were opened and emptied into bowls. I could tell when Mom prepared the nut bowl—the big wooden bowl gave a more mellow sound than the glass candy dishes. Since there were no screams of discovery, I figured I was safe and had gotten away with my crime scot-free. I rolled over, snuggled down under my comforter, and fell asleep.

The next morning we were up early. Donna woke first (she's *always* been a "morning person"), and within minutes she had Jim and me awake. We shrugged into our robes, pulled on our slippers, and raced downstairs. Mom was already up and had a fresh pot of coffee brewed. Dad was at least conscious, and looked like he would be fine after about two cups of coffee. Raymond was sitting in his highchair, finishing a bowl of cereal and a glass of milk. We assembled around the Christmas tree and waited impatiently for Mom to turn Raymond loose. One of the Christmas rules was that no one simply dived into the packages—we gathered as a family and took turns opening our gifts. Soon, Raymond pattered in from the dining room with Mom right behind him, and Christmas could start.

We began opening the packages, taking the time to express admiration and appreciation for each present. As the morning progressed, the rich smell of the roasting turkey wafted through the house and people began feeling hungry. This was when we could help ourselves to any of the assortment of goodies laid out. I was surreptitiously keeping an eye on the nut bowl, and Dad was the first one to crack open an empty walnut. He stared in disbelief at the empty shell in his hand and said, "Well, I'll be damned. Look at this—I've never seen anything like this before." He held out the empty shell for inspection.

Mom automatically murmured, "Language, Leonard." Then she glanced at what he was holding out. "Well, that is strange. Must have been a worm or something."

Dad re-examined the shell. "Well,...maybe. I guess you always get a couple of bad ones." He threw the shell in an empty box and selected another walnut. That one was fine. (It must have come from one of the bags of mixed nuts.) He laughed and said, "Now this is more like it. I do love walnuts!" He happily munched away, then cracked another one. Empty! In fact, so empty it looked as if it might have been vacuumed out. "Bernice! Look at this! It's another one."

Mom was sitting on the floor, involved in trying to show Raymond that you could do other things with Lincoln Logs than just throw them. She responded to Dad's outburst with a simple, questioning "Hm-m-m-m?"

"Look at this! It's another bad walnut! Where did you buy these?"

Now she looked up and saw another empty shell. Then Jim said, "Hey! I got one, too!" He also held out an empty shell for inspection.

Mom's brow wrinkled in confusion. "Oh, my," she said, "That *is* odd. I got them at the commissary, just like I always do. They're the same brand I always buy." She got up and went to the nut bowl, picking up several nuts that she proceeded to crack. They were all perfect. Of course they were—she had selected two pecans, a couple of filberts, and an almond. "These seem all right. Here, eat these." She handed the nuts to Dad.

Another yelp from Jim interrupted this idyllic scene, "Holy cow! It's another bad one."

Now, Donna grabbed a nutcracker and started popping open nuts. Since I didn't want to appear obvious, I got in on the action, too. I picked up the last nutcracker and a handful of filberts. It didn't take long for someone to notice that the problem of the empty nutshells seemed to center around walnuts. There was some speculation about a bad walnut crop that year, but no one seemed to be buying that as an explanation. Mom pointed out that the bags had been sealed, they had been hidden away, and she had opened them just hours before. It was a mystery, all right!

After this brief flurry of activity, everyone settled back down to Christmas. There were still some presents remaining to be opened, and there was nothing wrong with any of the other goodies. We proceeded with the morning, though I noticed that everyone seemed to be avoiding the remaining walnuts in the bowl. Certain that my plan had worked exactly, I relaxed my guard. I had gotten away with it!

Unfortunately, I had forgotten about my older brother's persistence, particularly when he was presented with a mystery. After all the packages were open and Mom had gone into the kitchen to baste the turkey, Jim began quietly picking up the walnut shells and examining them closely. While it was true that some of the walnuts had actually contained nuts, ninety percent of them had been empty. Jim was going to figure out why.

I was well into chapter one of my new book when Jim's voice cut through my awareness. "Hey!" he shouted, "These have *glue* on them!"

Dad asked, "What's that, Jim? Glue? Where?"

"On these walnuts! Look, you can see some of it right here where it oozed onto the shell." He brought one of the empty shells over to Dad and pointed out the traces of glue that he had found.

Dad took the shell and stared at it in utter confusion. He repeated, "Glue??"

Jim had grabbed some more of the empty shells and was scrutinizing them. "Yeah, glue! And look here. Here's some more on this one. And here's some more! Someone opened these, ate the nuts, and *glued them back together!*"

The ruckus had brought Mom back from the kitchen, and she also examined the shells. Then she shook her head and said, "But that's impossible. The bags were still sealed." Jim looked at Mom briefly, then slipped out of the living room.

"Well, I think we should send these back to the S&W Company with a letter of complaint," Dad said. "The nerve of them—selling empty nuts! I bet we could get a year's supply of nuts for free!"

I was making a great show of being as mystified as everyone else when Jim reappeared in the living room door, holding two of the empty walnut bags. He handed one of the bags to Dad and said, "No, Dad, these were opened and resealed. Look at it closely at the top. You can see where some of the cellophane melted, and that mark there looks like the tip of an iron."

Oh, great! I thought. I have to get Sherlock Holmes for a brother!

Mom now added the zinger. Looking around the room at each of us, she quietly said, "Now, who in the world would do something like that? And at Christmas, too."

Feigning innocence, I looked around the room, also. When my glance got to Donna, she was staring at me with a look of total suspicion. "Yeah," she said sarcastically, "*who in the world* would do something that low? Who likes nuts that much? Who's been sitting here all morning stuffing her face with filberts and pecans and not even touching the walnuts?" She didn't even blink, and now the stare had transformed into a glare.

Mom looked at me. I was blushing scarlet and knew that I was caught, but I bit my lip and held my silence hoping to bluff my way through. The room was silent as Mom continued to nail me with her "Mother Look", then she quietly asked, "Patty? Did you do this?"

My number was up, and I knew it. I started stammering, "Well, I...I..."

Dad had been staring at me in disbelief, and now he added, "She glued the nuts back together? How? When? I mean, she actually glued...? Oh, Lord, what is the matter with that child?"

That did it. I started crying and confessing at the same time. I'm not sure if everyone got all the details because of all the blubbering and sniffling going on throughout the confession, but they certainly got the gist of it. When I finished, I was hiccoughing and snuffling. Except for Raymond (who was too little to understand what was going on), everyone was staring at me like I had just sprouted a second head and purple horns.

After a few seconds that felt like hours, Mom said, "Well. I can't believe that I have to say this on *Christmas day* but, Patty, I think you need to spend a little time in the thinking chair. I'll be in the kitchen when you've figured it out."

I spent the requisite time in the thinking chair, then trudged into the kitchen. Since I couldn't replace the nuts, I figured that I owed everyone in the family an apology. Mom agreed, and then added three days of doing dishes just to make sure the lesson stuck. At Christmas dinner I stood up, apologized to everyone, and promised that I would leave the rest of the nuts for them. In the spirit of the season, my apology was graciously accepted.

The strangest result of the whole affair was that Dad spent Christmas afternoon in his chair, cracking open empty walnuts and examining the shells. Most of the time, he kept muttering, "How did she get 'em open so cleanly? Glue, for God's sake, glue! In the sewing room at midnight..."

Hey, St. Jude

...as told by Donna

The winter of 1955 was hard. It had set in early with the first snow coming during the last week in October. In fact, there was snow on the ground on Halloween, and we had to wear coats and snow pants under our costumes when we went "trick-'n-treating."

Being just ten years old, I didn't follow the weather patterns. All I knew was that it was cold and freezing-wet outside and, because of the situation, working my paper route had become more and more difficult as the days went by. Jim and I had to deal with the snow and ice the best possible way we knew. We couldn't ride our bikes on our paper route—that would have been more trouble than it was worth. The best solution to traversing the snow was to strap our paper-bags to our sleds and then to go it on foot. Mom bundled us up in multiple layers of clothing, along with very sensible and, in my opinion, very ugly snow boots. They were called "four-buckle-Arctics." These boots were made of thick black rubber, opened in the front, and closed with four unsightly metal buckles (there was no way our feet were going to get wet in those things). I did own a pair of red boots with fake fur around the top that I thought were very stylish, but Mom would let me wear them only to school and to church. The paper route called for something far more "practical."

To top off this winter fashion ensemble, Dad had decided to add one more stylish touch. Sunset came early in Illinois during the winter, around five o'clock or five thirty. We were still delivering our papers at that time. We were on foot and our clothing was dark colored—sometimes we were hard to see by on-coming cars. To avoid any unfortunate accident, Dad marked us front and back with large X's, using silver-coated military reflecting tape. There was no way anyone on the Paxton roads was going to miss seeing us. In fact, we were probably visible to any beings inhabiting any nearby planets.

*   *   *

School had let out for the Christmas vacation and it was the last Friday before Christmas. Boy, did I love that day! Friday was "collection day" on our paper route. The weekly paper cost 20 cents. Out of that 20 cents we made a profit of 12 cents per customer. The other 8 cents was our inventory cost and was paid to the newspaper publisher. Christmas was the exception. On the last collection before Christmas the customer gave the paperboy (or, as in my case, the papergirl) a customary Christmas gift. It was much easier for most people to just give us extra money than try to figure out what to buy for a child who was basically a stranger. Custom proved to be either 50 cents or a dollar tip. Wow! The money just seemed to flow! Of course, there were the few customers who would always give us those little boxes that looked like a book and contained ten rolls of Life Savers™. I liked the cherry ones, the multi-flavored ones and the butterscotch ones. However as far as I was concerned, they could have left out the peppermint and wintergreen; these two flavors I generously shared with my family by putting them in the Christmas candy bowl.

Because it seemed impossible for me to save any money throughout the year (some basic flaw in our monetary structure that has yet to be properly addressed by the Feds), I depended on my paper route tips to buy Christmas gifts for my family. That Friday before the holiday had a dual meaning for me. Not only did it represent a bonus for working hard, but it also saved me the embarrassment of not being able to participate in the family gift giving.

The tips were very generous that year. I believe it may have been because that winter was so hard. On that Friday the weather was exceptionally bad. It had sleeted the evening before and then turned to snow during the night. There was a good six inches of snow on the ground, covering about an inch of solid ice. I not only wore the standard snow gear that afternoon, but I also had on two pairs of socks and two pairs of gloves.

I dutifully packed my newspapers, strapped them to my sled and headed out into the elements. Boy, was it cold! I thought I'd never make it through delivering all those papers and collecting payments, as well. What kept me going was the Christmas money. Because of the awful weather, many of my customers were sympathetic to my plight and gave me a "little more than usual." I, of course, displayed what I thought was a very cold and suffering demeanor. The money was handed to me accompanied by a concerned look and a "you poor child" or "oh my, you poor thing" comment. It was great! My moneybag weighed a ton! It was going to be a generous Christmas that year. Not only would I have enough money to buy all my Christmas gifts, but there would also be extra left over for me to squander on myself.

The money was well earned as I trekked through the ankle-deep snow and maneuvered on the icy streets. The town had dispatched the snowplows early that morning. The streets had been scraped clear of the snow, but the blades on the plows couldn't break through the ice. As a result, the roads were left in a very slippery, treacherous state.

There was one particular street on my paper route that ran up a very steep hill. I couldn't stay on my feet as I tried to walk to the top. I had customers up and down this hill, and could not avoid it. I slipped and bruised my rump several times trying to ascend it. But, being fiercely determined, I decided to put the rope of my sled around my waist and crawl on my hands and knees to the top of the hill, pulling my sled behind me. Going down would not be as treacherous; I had decided to start at the top of the hill and then zigzag from side to side of the street, stopping at all my customers' houses on the way down. It wasn't a bad plan, and after I got to the top it worked fairly well.

The only huge problem I encountered occurred on the first time I crawled up that hill (yes, I said "the first time"). It was slow going and took me a long time to get to the top. I had almost reached my goal when the rope around my waist slipped down to my knees. It all happened in a few seconds. I was crawling at a steady pace; the rope slipped and I crawled right over it before I could stop. My sled and all my papers went flying down that icy hill and didn't come to rest until it reached the curb at the bottom. I turned around and just sat there as my sled went AWOL. The downward distance of that street seemed like miles to me, and my sled looked very small parked at the bottom.

Tears started to well in my eyes, but then I remembered Mom telling us that tears could freeze to your face in very cold weather, taking the skin with them when they melted. I sucked in my breath, stopped the tears before they flowed, and in defiance shouted, "Damn it!" That was forbidden language, but I had said it anyway, and I was glad that I did. That one loud curse gave me the gumption to push off on my bottom and slide all the way down the hill to my sled. The second time I secured the sled rope around my waist by pulling it through the third button hole on my coat. I made it to the top of the hill and successfully back down. As I headed home, I honestly thought that I had overcome the worst that could have happened to me that day.

The trip home took at least another half-hour. I stayed clear of the icy roads and trekked through the snow across people's lawns instead of testing my balance on those nasty streets. The snow had drifted on several of the lawns and at times I found myself high-stepping through at least eight to ten inches of snow. When I finally arrived home, I was exhausted, wet, and cold. I put my sled up, and then trudged up the back stairs into the house. Mom was waiting for me with a large cup of hot chocolate—the perfect remedy for a cold, aching little ten-year-old body. I was still carrying my paper-bag. It was weighed down with my moneybag and the three extra papers we were required to carry to replace any that might "accidentally" fall in a mud puddle or land on the top of someone's roof.

I plopped down onto a dining room chair and dropped my bag to the floor at my side. When my paper-bag hit the linoleum surface, it made a soft "thud" sound. There was no jingling of coins when it hit. I froze in place (that is not a pun) and listened intently, as though the jingling sound might be delayed. Nothing but silence occurred in those next few critical seconds. "Oh, no!" I cried. I jumped off my chair and grabbed my paper-bag all in one motion. I knelt down, frantically emptying the bag. Three extra papers and a couple of those Life Saver™ books were the only contents of my paper-bag! I turned the bag upside down, shaking it furiously and hoping my moneybag might just mysteriously drop out. It didn't. I just kept saying, "Oh, no!" over and over again.

Mom heard me (how could she *not* have heard my pitiful moaning?) and came into the dining room. "What's wrong, Donna?" she asked.

"I lost my moneybag!" I wailed. "Oh, my God, it's gone! All my money is *gone!*"

"Now, calm down," she said softly. "Where was your moneybag?"

I looked up at her with wide eyes as though she was speaking to me in some foreign language. How could she be so calm and collected when my whole being was shattered?

She knelt down beside me and, in the same calm voice, asked, "Was your moneybag in your paper-bag?"

I just nodded my head in assent and kept looking into her concerned face. *She will help me,* I thought, *and everything will be all right.*

"Now, stand up, Donna, and sit in the chair. Let's try to figure this out," she said, as she helped me to my feet. That's when I started to cry. Through gulps and sobs, I told her about my afternoon on my paper route. I told her everything: how bad the roads were, how I had to crawl up the hill, how I had to deal with a runaway sled, how hard it was to walk through the snow drifts, and how very cold and tired I was.

When I was finished, we both sat there in silence for a minute or two. Then Mom said, "You must have lost it after you were through collecting, right?"

"Yes," I replied. "I got all my collecting done, and put my moneybag in my paper-bag like I always do."

Mother didn't say a word. I could see she was thinking.

"It must have slipped out," I added in a very low voice.

"What was the last house you collected from?" she asked.

"The last place I stopped at was the Reynolds' house, and then headed home."

"See there!" Mom said brightly. "That's not that far from here! You lost your moneybag somewhere between our house and theirs, and that's less than a half mile! I'd bet next week's milk money that you could find that moneybag in no time at all."

"What?" I exclaimed. "How am I going to do that? It's already dark outside, and freezing cold!"

"You want to find your moneybag, don't you?" she asked. I silently nodded my head in agreement. "Okay," she continued, "Dad will be home in about thirty minutes. I'll ask him to take the car and drop you off at the Reynolds' house. From there you need to backtrack your route home. Walk back exactly the way you went earlier. Don't change your path even a little bit. I know you will find your moneybag."

She said all of that with a great deal of confidence—in fact, a lot more confidence than I had. "How do you know I'll find my money?" I challenged.

"I know you will because, after you finish drinking your hot chocolate, both you and I are going to get down on our knees and say a prayer to St. Jude."

"What?" I asked incredulously. "Who's St. Jude? And why are we gonna pray to him?"

"St. Jude is the patron saint of lost causes and lost items. We will ask him to walk by your side on your way back home and help you to find your moneybag. I just know he will answer our prayers."

I wasn't quite sure I believed in this St. Jude she was talking about, but I didn't have any other plan or answer to my problem. I didn't want to go back out into that icy night, but what else could I do? I asked meekly, "Could we pray and ask *him* to go out and find my moneybag while I stay home in this nice, warm house?"

"You know it doesn't work like that, Donna. You have to find your own moneybag, but St. Jude will be there to guide you."

"I don't know how you expect me to find my moneybag in that deep snow, in the dark!"

"Honey, please have a little faith in yourself and in St. Jude," she said quietly. "You *can* find your moneybag." With that final affirmation Mom went to her room. I sat there staring at my cup of hot chocolate as the realization of the task before me poked at my brain.

Mom returned to the dining room carrying her favorite prayer book. Believe it or not, there was a defined prayer to St. Jude in there. I got up from my chair and stood by its side. Mom and I knelt down together, each on opposing sides of the chair. She opened her prayer book and read aloud the prayer to St. Jude. When she finished the prayer she said, "Now let's silently say a prayer of our own to St. Jude to help you find your moneybag." She bowed her head and closed her eyes. I did the same. I really didn't know what to say to this saint, so I just knelt there with hands folded and head bent, hoping for the best.

As we were getting up from our kneeling position, the door to the basement opened and Jim entered the room. He had a very bewildered look on his face and started to say, "What..."

Before he could get his sentence out, I said, "I lost my moneybag and gotta find it.... St. Jude and all."

"Oh," he softly said, and nodded his head in understanding. Then he added, "Wow, what a bummer! Do ya' want me to go with you and keep you company?"

"No," I said, a little downhearted. "It's not gonna do any good for both of us to get cold and wet again. Besides, I gotta do this on my own."

"Yeah, I know," he sympathized, then turned and went upstairs to his room.

Dad got home about ten minutes later. Mom and I were still in the dining room. I was just standing there, cooperating but not helping as Mom worked at bundling me up to face the wet and cold again.

"It's as cold as a brass monkey's ass in a snow storm out there!" Dad announced as he entered the room.

"Leonard!" Mom admonished, as she did every time he said a swear word or used "bad" language. I didn't look up at him. I just stood there with my head down.

"What's up?" Dad asked Mom.

"Oh, Donna lost her moneybag on the way home tonight and needs to go back out and try to find it," she informed him.

"You didn't have it stuffed inside your coat like I told you to do, did you?" he asked me.

"No," I answered very quietly and slightly rebuffed.

"I told you once, if not a thousand times, this was going to happen if you didn't zip that bag inside your jacket. Well, you lost it—you gotta find it!" he decreed.

I still didn't look at him. I said nothing to his comment, but I did think *"Meany."* It took years and years to pass before I realized that my Dad really did care, but didn't know how to express himself. He told me, much later in time, that it had just about killed him to take me back out into that weather and drop me off at the Reynolds' house. But that didn't help me back then.

On the way to the Reynolds', I didn't say a word, but just sat in the passenger's seat of the car with my head hung low. I could feel my dad looking over at me several times during our trip, but he didn't say anything either. When I got out of the car and turned to close the door, Dad just said, "Good luck, Donna." He reached under the driver's seat and pulled out his big military flashlight. Handing it to me, he said, "This will help. Just go slow and easy."

I stood on the Reynolds' lawn and watched as Dad slowly drove away. I didn't move until I lost sight of the car's taillights. I was all alone in the dark and cold. It was like I was brain-dead, and couldn't understand what I was doing there. Then a thought bumped my poor confused head—*Mom said I wouldn't be alone because St. Jude was going to walk with me.* I looked up and measured the path I needed to take to start my hunt. It really wasn't that dark outside. There was a big moon that reflected off the snow and really lit up the night. I could clearly see my footprints in the snow where I had walked earlier that evening. For the first time since I realized I had lost my money, I began to feel hopeful.

I picked out my starting point, and, as I walked towards it, swinging my flashlight gently back and forth on the ground, I said out loud, "Okay, St. Jude, it's you and me, buddy. No slacking off—heads bent and eyes to the ground!" I determinedly took my first step forward.

As I marched along my own trail, eyes glued to the ground, I kept talking to St. Jude. I asked him what he looked like and how old he was. Was he married and did he have any kids. I wanted to know what he had done to be put in charge of God's lost and found department. I told him all about my lousy day, and then explained about all the gifts I needed to buy and how important that money was to me. We walked together and talked together as we slowly trudged through the snow with my eyes never leaving the path.

After approximately twenty minutes had passed, I stopped and looked up. I was more than half way home and hadn't found my moneybag yet. A little bit of panic started to set in—the blocks were slipping behind me one by one, and I still hadn't found my money.

"I hope you're still with me, St. Jude," I said aloud. "I'm running out of ground here, and still no luck. Would you be mad at me if I asked you for a little miracle, or at least some kind of sign that we're working together on this problem?"

I stood still and listened intently, but heard no answer. It was hard for me to take the next necessary step to get started again. In my mind I silently prayed, *"Please, please, St. Jude, help me. I promise to light a candle to you and double my church donation for one month, if you will help me now!"*

I started to count my steps—one, two, three, etc. It kept my mind and my eyes concentrated. On the sixth step my foot hit a large obstacle under the snow. It could have been a sizable rock or tree branch or whatever. I didn't see it at all. My big toe, in spite of the thick layers of socks, screamed "ouch!" as it made contact with this object. I couldn't keep my balance and landed face first in the snow. I lay there while my toe throbbed. I pushed the snow away from my face and laid my forehead on my folded forearms. I really believed that I could not take any more bad luck. I just wanted to get up and start yelling at the top of my lungs that this wasn't fair. Instead, with a heavy sigh, I started to push myself up into a kneeling position.

As I was beginning to lift up, my left hand slipped a little to the side of where it was braced. When I started to pull my hand back, I felt something under the snow that was not supposed to be there. I knelt up rapidly and brushed the snow aside. There, poking out of the little snowdrift, was the corner of my blue moneybag! I knelt there staring at it, almost afraid that it wasn't real.

"It IS your moneybag, Dummy!"

I went into action, scooping the snow away in big wet handfuls. It was indeed my moneybag. I snatched it out of the snow and hugged it to my chest. "I found it! I found it!" I began to holler. I hope the only person who heard me was St. Jude. Anyone else would have thought I had gone nuts.

I jumped up and began dancing around in a circle, still hugging my moneybag. I stopped when I started to become breathless.

"Hey, St. Jude," I shouted, "Let's make a snow angel to celebrate!" I zipped my moneybag into my snow jacket, and then plopped down on my back in a patch of undisturbed snow. I flapped my arms and legs simultaneously to make the wings and skirt of my snow angel. When done, I carefully stood up within the imprint on the snow and stepped out of it. I turned to appraise my artwork. It was a perfect angel. I walked around to the bottom of the figure, knelt down, and wrote "ST. JUDE" in the snow.

The rest of the way home went very quickly. I half walked and half ran, not caring where I trod. I burst into the house, ecstatic. "I found it! I really found it!" I yelled, waving my moneybag in the air. Everyone was patting me on the back and expressing their good feelings for me all at once. The family had waited dinner for me, and supper time that night was animated with conversation and stories about lost things. It was a happy ending to a very hard day.

Later that night I went out to the kitchen to find Mom. For some reason I needed to be with her and talk awhile. I started helping her cut up apples for a pie she was going to bake the next day.

"Mom?" I asked, "I think St. Jude was with me tonight. I can't explain it, but I know I wasn't alone. Does that make any sense to you?"

"Honey," she said softly, "if you believe St. Jude was with you, then he was. That is the essence of faith."

We both became quiet and continued slicing up the apples. As I silently worked beside my mother, I thought about how really neat it was to have a bona fide saint as my friend.

I did light that candle for St. Jude, and I doubled my church donation for the next month. It was the least I could do for a good trooper like him.

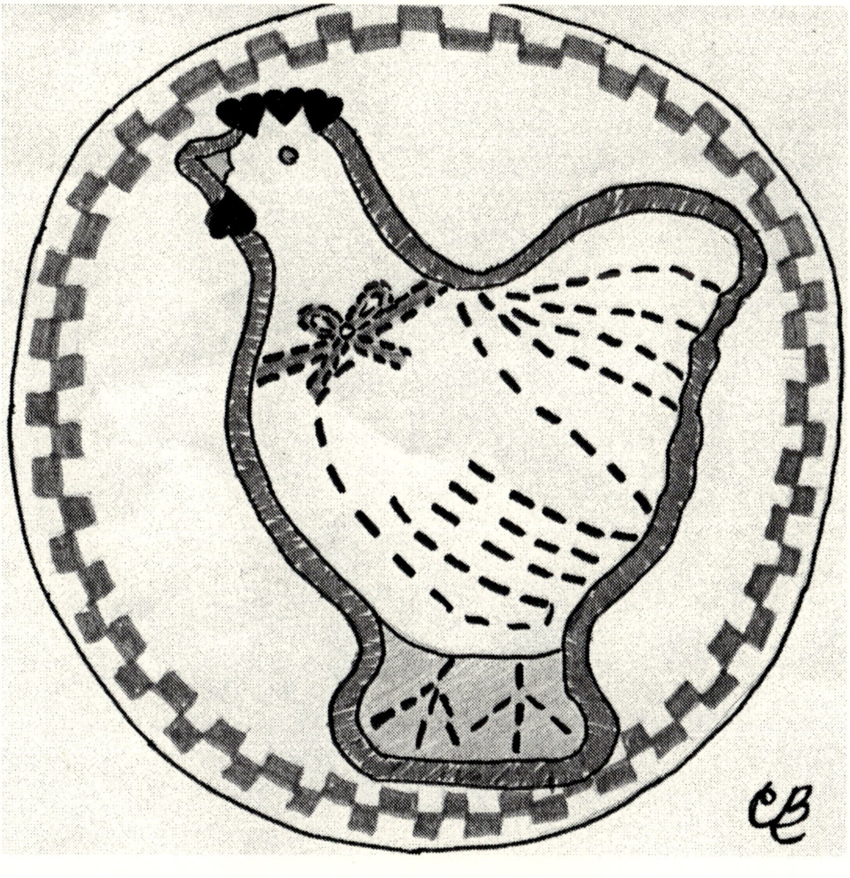
CB

And a Chicken in a Pear Tree

...as told by Pat

"All right, kids, everything's ready. Time to play Christmas elves and help get these cookies frosted."

It was the signal we had been waiting for. We piled into the dining room and spread out around the table, one to each side. The table was covered with newspaper with long strips of waxed paper on top. Bottles of colored sugar sprinkles, cinnamon red-hots, chocolate dashes, and other decorations were distributed within easy reach, and bowls of colored frosting were set at each side of the table. In the center, Mom had placed the big turkey platter, but today it held a mountain of sugar cookies cut in Christmas shapes.

Mom pulled Raymond's highchair up to one side of the table and said, "This year, I'm going to let Raymond help. I think he's old enough to start learning to decorate cookies, and I want you other three to help him if he needs it."

She reached down and lifted my two-year-old brother into his chair, and then scooted him up close to the table. Raymond was so excited, he was wiggling all over. Mom gave him the small butter knife, placed some custard cups of frosting within his reach, and added several cookies. She showed him how to scoop up some frosting and spread it on a cookie, then handed him the butter knife and left him to it.

Mom surveyed the table one last time. We each had a stack of cookies and were busily decorating them. "Okay," she said, "I have some packages to wrap, so I'll be in the bedroom. Have fun."

For the next few minutes, silence reigned in the dining room as we concentrated on our task. We frosted cookies, added sprinkles or decorations as the mood moved us, and then lined the finished cookies up on the waxed paper to dry.

The silence was broken when Jim said, "Hey, cool. Look at this." He held up a reindeer that was a sickly shade of lavender with green antlers and a bright red cinnamon red-hot serving as the eye. In a spooky, hollow voice he added, "Oo-o-o-e-e-eo-o-o-o. It came from outer space." He and Donna burst into laughter.

"How did you get purple?" Donna asked.

"I just mixed up a little of the blue and the red. See?" Jim pointed at a small scrap of waxed paper with a blob of purple frosting. "Let's see, how about a purple Christmas tree?" He grabbed a tree-shaped cookie and smeared purple all over it.

I had observed this quietly, then gave a little sniff of disapproval. Purple reindeer and trees, indeed! In my opinion, Jim was being silly. I preferred *art verité*, where trees were green, stars were yellow, and angels, of course, were white. Since we didn't have any brown frosting, I avoided the reindeer. I collected another handful of cookies and carefully began decorating them *correctly*, while at the other end of the table, Donna and Jim were now mixing up a veritable rainbow of colors.

My concentration was broken by my sister's voice. "Raymie! Stop that! Use the knife that Mom gave you!"

I glanced at my little brother. The butter knife had been abandoned, and he was dipping his fingers into the cups of frosting and then smearing it on his cookies. He would then lick his fingers clean before dipping up some more frosting. Frosting was pretty liberally smeared all around his place at the table, as well as on his face, shirt, and arms. I sat back to watch what would happen next.

Donna stepped over to him, picked up the butter knife, and handed it to him. Taking his hand in hers, she began showing him how to do it. "Now, see, Raymie? You take the *knife* to get the frosting and spread it. Okay? Now, you try it."

Raymond looked up at Donna, placed the knife on the table, licked his fingers and then very deliberately stuck them in the frosting.

"Oh, yuck! No, no, no—use the knife." Donna moved the butter knife close to Raymond's hand.

Raymond looked at the knife for a moment, then pushed it away and scooped up more frosting.

"How are things going in here with the cookies?" Mom asked as she walked into the dining room.

Donna put her hands on her hips and heaved a huge, exasperated sigh. "Raymie is being absolutely disgusting," she announced.

"Really?" replied Mom, "And what does a two-year-old do to be so disgusting?"

"He won't use his knife. He's *finger-painting* his cookies, and he keeps sticking his fingers in his mouth!"

Mom looked at Raymond and his cookies. He was again sucking frosting off his fingers in preparation for scooping up more. His cookies were a multi-colored swirl spread out in front of him.

"Believe it or not, there was a time when all of you finger-painted cookies, too, and licked your fingers. So far, nobody has died from eating the cookies."

Donna snorted in disbelief. "I never did that," she announced.

Mom thought for a moment and then replied, "Actually, dear, you're probably right. I can't imagine *you* sticking *your fingers* in anything as gooey as frosting. Look, let's do this. Raymond can frost his cookies however he wants, and we'll set those cookies aside for him to eat. All right?"

"Oh, I guess so, but it's still disgusting." Donna moved back to her place and picked up a cookie.

I picked up another cookie and started to decide how to decorate it. It was a large cookie in the shape of a bird, and I immediately recognized it. It was a chicken. I had helped Mrs. Nelson gather eggs and feed her chickens often enough that I knew exactly what a chicken looked like. I looked over my decorating supplies and smiled. This cookie would be a masterpiece!

First, I applied a smooth coating of white frosting. Next, using just the tip of my knife, I used yellow for the beak and feet. Cinnamon red-hots made a perfect crest and wattle, and a silvery candy b-b served as the eye. I looked at my chicken critically. More detail was needed. Shaking out some chocolate dashes, I used a toothpick to carefully arrange them, outlining the wing, separating the tail feathers, and making toes. Bent closely over my cookie, tongue clamped between my teeth, I was intent on making this a perfect portrait. Finally, using green frosting, I put a Christmas bow on its neck, and once again used the chocolate dashes to outline the loops and ties of the bow.

A last, critical examination assured me there was nothing more to be added. I carefully turned the cookie around, picked it up by the edges, and held it up for display. "Hey, look at this. What do you think?"

Donna and Jim looked over, and there was silence for a few seconds. Then Donna said, "Is that what I think it is? A chicken? You made a *Christmas Chicken?*"

I nodded. "Yeah! It's a chicken. Isn't that what it's supposed to be?"

"Um-m-m-m, Twerp, I think that's supposed to be a partridge," added Jim.

"A partridge?" I asked.

"Yeah, you know, like a partridge in a pear tree?"

Donna was laughing out loud now. "A Christmas Chicken! Dum-dum made a Christmas *Chicken!*"

Oh, no! I had done it wrong! I put my chicken down and stared at it for a few seconds. Then I looked up and asked, "What's a partridge look like?"

"Well, first of all, they're brown."

I could feel myself deflate. Not only had I done it wrong; I had also done it horribly wrong! Wrong bird, wrong color, and I suddenly suspected that partridges did not have crests and wattles.

Donna and Jim, however, now both had a case of the giggles, and began having a lot of fun at my expense.

"Hey! We can start a new tradition. The Christmas Chicken!"

"Yeah, let's see, it comes down the chimney on Christmas morning and crows to wake everyone up."

"That would be a Christmas Rooster! The Christmas Chicken would have to lay a Christmas Egg!"

"Okay, so it comes down the chimney, lays a huge egg, and clucks. Then, Dad grabs it, and—uur-r-r-r-ck—we've got the main item for Christmas dinner!" (A very realistic wringing motion of Jim's hands accompanied this comment.) Donna and Jim collapsed in their chairs, laughing so hard they could barely gasp out their observations.

In disgust, I picked up my chicken and knife.

"What are you doing to that cookie now?" asked Donna. "You just spent an hour decorating it."

"I'm going to scrape it off and start over."

"Oh, geez Louise, don't be so dumb! We've still got a pile of cookies to do. Put it aside and do another one."

"No, this one's wrong, and I gotta fix it."

"What do you need to fix, honey?" Mom had just entered the room.

"This cookie. It's messed up."

"What? This cookie?" Mom slid the chicken out from under my hovering knife. "Why, that's a lovely cookie. Whatever in the world do you think is wrong with it?"

"It's a chicken."

"Yes, it is. I noticed that right away. What's wrong with it?"

"It's s'posed to be a partridge."

"Really? Why does it need to be a partridge?"

"Jim said it's not s'posed to be a chicken. It's s'posed to be a partridge."

Mom glanced at the end of the table where Jim and Donna, still snickering, were busily engaged frosting cookies. "Well, let's see now." She reached over to the pile of cookies, selected another bird-shaped one, and studied it carefully. Then she laid it on the table next to me.

"I don't see anything on here that says it has to be a partridge. Do you?"

I glanced at the fresh cookie. "No."

Mom continued, "All I see is a bird, and it could be any kind of bird at all. It might be a cardinal or a blue jay; they stay here all winter. Maybe it's a pheasant, or a turkey, or *even* a chicken. What do you think?"

"But, Jim said it was a partridge, like a partridge in a pear tree. You know, like the song?"

"Well, it *could* be a partridge, but it could just as easily be something else. You see, that's the nice thing about your imagination—it has no limits. When Jim looked at this, he saw a partridge; when you looked at it, you saw a chicken. And you used your imagination to decorate it as a very nice chicken. I don't see anything wrong with that."

"Well-l-l, I guess it's okay…"

"It's more than okay. In fact, may I have this cookie?"

"Huh? Oh, sure, but why?"

"Because I like it and think it's a special cookie. I'm going to set it here to dry, and I don't want anyone else to eat it. This is my special Christmas cookie, and I'm going to save it for Christmas morning."

Jim added, "Yeah, Twerp, it's a cool chicken, and, if you think about it for a minute, a Christmas Chicken is pretty funny."

"Yeah, but I didn't make fun of your stupid purple reindeer."

Jim grinned. "My purple *outer space* reindeer. And, we weren't making fun of *you*. It was just that the Christmas Chicken was so funny."

I thought about it, and found the corners of my lips twitching up into a little smile. A chicken waking everyone up on Christmas morning *was* pretty funny, after all.

Mom took control of the situation once more. "All right, now, there are still a lot of cookies to be frosted, and we need to get them done and the table cleaned up before dinner. Let's have fun with this, and remember that they're just cookies." She looked around the table at all of us, then quietly left the room.

We got busy, and after about an hour the cookies were all done. We ended up with the usual array of rainbow colors, bright sparkles, and strange details. (The reindeer whose front leg had broken off had a neat sling to compensate.) No matter what they looked like, they still tasted wonderful and were an important part of our Christmas.

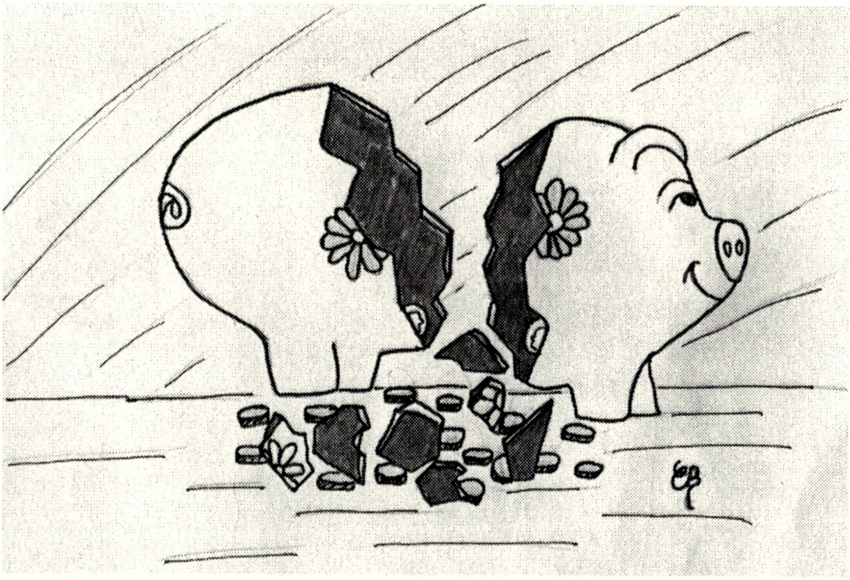

If You Haven't Got a Ha'penny, Then God Bless You

...as told by Donna

I went over my Christmas shopping list one more time, checking my math and making sure my choices were final. I was going to buy Jim the Chinese Checkers game he wanted (cost $2.98). I was going to get Pat the new black stallion paperback book (cost $1.50), and for Ray a set of baby A-B-C blocks made out of plastic instead of wood so he could chew on them (cost 98 cents). Dad wanted a new key chain (cost $3.99), and Mom needed a new pair of garden gloves (cost $2.99). This all added up to $12.44, and then there would be sales tax too. I rounded the amount up to an estimated $13.00. I had saved $17.50, which still left me $4.50 for buying Christmas cards or any other unseen item I had overlooked.

For me to save $17.50 was no small task. I was one of those children whose money always came and went very quickly, but I wanted that trend to change. Back in August I made myself start saving a small amount each week from my paper route money. I had been dearly tempted during the last several weeks to "borrow from my fund," but had managed to control myself. I was proud and pleased with my newfound discipline.

The last two years I had to borrow money from Jim to complete my Christmas gift purchases. He was not a gentle lender. I had to pay him back a portion of my loan each Friday (no excuses allowed) until the principal amount was covered, and then on top of that he made me pay him *interest*. Even when I accused him of having the middle name of Scrooge, he would not relent on the interest. Well, I had made up my mind that I was not going to repeat that humility anymore. It was the last week in November, and I had more than enough money to really enjoy my Christmas shopping.

I had been lying on my stomach on my bed as I *checked my list twice*. I rolled over, hands behind my head and thought to myself, "eleven years old, and I have a small fortune. Oh boy, I love shopping with no stress." To add to my sense of accomplishment, I jumped up and decided to count my money again. I had put it in the bottom tray of my jewelry box; dollar bills clipped together with a hairpin and two quarters laid on top. I was humming *We Wish You a Merry Christmas* as I went to retrieve my hard earned moola (as Dad would call it).

It was gone! My money wasn't in my jewelry box! Oh my God, where was my money!? I started moving everything on top of my dresser, and then began going through every drawer. My money wasn't there! As panic set in, my actions became more and more frantic. How could I have lost my money? Every time I counted it, I always put it back in the same place. How could it just disappear?

I plunked down on the edge of my bed. I needed to think, but rationality had left me. I jumped up again and checked my jewelry box. Maybe, just maybe, I had been temporarily blind when I looked in it the first time. No such luck—the money was definitely gone. *Somebody stole it*. That was the only answer—somebody must have stolen my money!

Then the horror of that thought struck me. It had to be either Jim or Pat who took my money. How could they do that to me? I was going to buy their gifts with that money. Oh dear, what was I going to do? This was a bigger crisis than I could handle alone. I ran downstairs to find Mom.

She was in the sewing room mending stuff. I rushed in and announced, "Somebody stole my money!"

"Ouch!" she said as she stuck herself with a straight pin. (I guess I must have startled her.)

"What?" she asked, looking up at me with consternation.

"Pat or Jim stole my Christmas money. I had $17.50 for Christmas presents. I kept it in the bottom drawer of my jewelry box, and now it's gone! One of them took it!"

"Where did you get $17.50?" Mom asked, a little incredulous.

"I saved it, for Pete's sake." I said defensively. "Are you listening to me? Pat or Jim stole my money! One of them is a thief!"

"Hold on, Donna. Aren't you jumping to conclusions?"

"I looked everywhere, and my money is not in my room. It can't just evaporate. One of them must have stolen it. Boy, how low can a person get?"

"Now wait a minute. Are you sure you looked *everywhere*? Mom inquired. "You know how bad you are at misplacing things."

"I didn't misplace it!" (My voice started rising) "I was very careful with that money! It was my Christmas money! Why are you blaming me for losing it?"

"I'm not *blaming* anyone, including your brother or sister. Let's go upstairs and thoroughly look again. We just might find it this time, especially if you say a little prayer to St. Jude (the patron saint of lost items) as we walk up to your room."

With that she stood up, took my hand and proceeded to the scene of the crime. We didn't say a word until we reached my room because we were *saying our little prayer*. Well, I really didn't say a prayer, just Mom did. I felt she had enough heavenly clout to pull that across on her own. Besides, I was still too upset to think about anything except the dastardly act of one of my siblings.

Mom and I covered every inch of my room. It took us over an hour to take everything out of the dresser and put it back, check every inch of the closet, look under the bed and behind the dresser, and inspect my bed coverings. The toy box was emptied, all the pockets on my clothes were investigated, and even the books in the bookcase were leafed through. No money was found (*Great job, St. Jude!*).

Again, I sat on the edge of my bed totally dejected. With watery eyes, I asked Mom, "Well, what now?"

"Well, you are right. Money doesn't just evaporate into thin air," she said. "If you are one hundred percent certain that you did not spend it, I will find out what happened to your money."

"I didn't spend it, Mom, I promise. It was too important to me," I said in a quiet, defeated voice.

"All right, I believe you. I will get to the bottom of this, but you have to give me a little time. I don't want you running to Jim or Pat and accusing them of stealing your money. Remember what I have always told you. Words, good or bad, once said, cannot be taken back, and you have to live with the results."

"Okay," I agreed.

"Why don't you lie down until dinner, and just quietly re-think about the last time you saw your money and where it might be. It never hurts to go over things one more time. I'll call you when it's time to eat."

When I came down for dinner I plunked myself in my chair and didn't say a word to anyone. I just sat there, with my head hanging down. I had no appetite at all.

"What's wrong with her?" Dad asked Mom in regards to my actions.

"Donna has a problem that concerns all of us, and we will discuss it after we eat. No one leaves this table tonight until we have all talked," Mom declared.

I looked up at her a little surprised. (She gently smiled back at me.) This was really unusual. Mom rarely called a *family meeting*—it was always Dad's job to do that. I looked around the table and saw the same shared reaction from the other members of the family, except Raymond. He was only one and a half years old, and had no concern in the world except to see how many green beans he could drop to the floor before Mom could stop him.

I looked over at my mother again. She was busy protecting Raymond's green beans, and everyone else was starting to pass the food dishes around the table. I felt this incredible respect and love for her. In spite of all the differences that existed between my mother and me, I could always, and I mean always, count on her.

After we were through eating, everyone stayed at his or her place. Mom explained about my lost money and why she needed to talk to all of them. She detailed all the places we looked, and re-confirmed that she believed that I had not spent it. Dad interrupted once to ask me if I had planned to go Christmas shopping so soon. I told him that I had been working on my gift list, and had checked to make sure I had enough money for the intended purchases. He nodded his head up and down in understanding.

Then we all listened quietly as Mom expressed her view on the eighth commandment "Thou Shall Not Steal." She ended her talk by saying, "I know that sometimes, especially when it seems to be an answer to an important need, a person can be tempted to do something they really don't want to do, but they do it anyway. Keep in mind, though, that the real issue here is how hard Donna worked for and saved that money, and no one has any right to it but her. I want you all to think very hard about what I've said. If you took the money, you must tell Donna tonight. She is very upset over this matter, and it isn't fair that she has to go to bed still worrying about it. I'm sure you wouldn't want to be in her shoes. I also know that it's hard to confess, but it is the only right thing to do. Enough said for now. I believe we all have some soul searching to do." She stood up and left the table, and so did the rest of us.

It was my turn to do the dishes that night. I had cleared off the table and was pouring a sinkful of hot, soapy water when Jim came into the kitchen. "Want some help?" he asked.

"Not really," I said with hostility.

"I know you're mad at Patty and me, but I didn't take your money, and, I believe, she didn't either."

"Then who did?" I asked.

"It could be someone you would least suspect," Jim said matter-of-factly.

"Oh, right," I replied sarcastically, "It was probably Raymond. He crawled out of his crib in the middle of the night and climbed up the stairs to steal my money. Who knows, he might have it stashed in his diapers right now as we speak."

"All right," Jim said in resignation. "You can stew in your suspicions for the rest of the night and make all the unfounded accusations you want to, but that won't bring back your money. I guess there's no talking to you while you're in a hateful mood." He turned and left the room.

I stared after him and thought, "Okay, Mister Know-It-All, you think what you want, and I'll think what I want!" I turned and started washing the dishes. I wondered, though, what he had meant by *the last person I would suspect*. It was beyond me, so I turned my thoughts again to which one of them had taken my money.

After I finished the dishes, I went into the living room and watched some TV by myself until it was time to get ready for bed. That night, instead of watching television with me, Dad had worked on some project in the basement the whole time I was still up. Maybe he wanted to be absent when the guilty person came to tell me they had taken my money. It was all for naught, because no one came to confess, and I went to bed that night still feeling betrayed.

I didn't say a word to my sister. After my bath, I went into our room, climbed into my bed and laid with my back to her. She turned out the light and climbed into her bed. "I didn't take your money, sincerely," she said in almost a whisper. I heard her, but pretended I was asleep.

It was around 10:30 and I was still awake, lying in bed staring at the ceiling. I had heard Mom and Dad talking earlier, but couldn't make out what they were saying. Then I distinctly heard Mom say "good-night" to Dad and close their bedroom door. About ten minutes later, Dad came upstairs. He stood in the open door of my bedroom and softly asked, "Donna, are you still awake?"

"Yes," I replied quietly.

"Why don't you come downstairs for a little while. I would like to talk to you."

"Okay," I agreed. As I got out of bed and slipped on my bathrobe, I glanced over at Pat and she appeared to be asleep, but I wasn't sure. I followed Dad downstairs.

He pulled out a chair at the dining room table for me to sit on, and then took his usual place. I noticed he had already fixed a cup of coffee for himself. It was sitting there cooling off waiting for him when we sat down. He looked at me and asked, "Would you like something to drink?"

"No, I don't think so. What did you want to talk to me about?" For some reason he seemed nervous and uncomfortable. I wondered why.

"Kind of a rough day, huh?"

"Yeah," I softly responded.

"Sometimes life gets pretty tough…even at Christmas time," he said.

I didn't answer him. I just nodded my head in agreement.

Dad sighed heavily, and then reached into his pant pocket and took out a small bunch of folded dollar bills. "Here, it's eighteen dollars to replace your lost money." he said as he held the cash out for me to take.

"I can't take your money!" I cried. "That's not right! The person who stole my money needs to replace it!"

There were a few second of silence. Then, "That's what that person is trying to do," he said hoarsely.

I couldn't believe I really heard what he had said. "What! Did you say that you stole my money!" I cried. "You're just trying to make things right for me, aren't you? You really didn't take my money, did you?" I looked directly into his eyes and held my breath. I wanted him to say he was only trying to help, and I wanted to see that truth in his eyes.

Dad lowered his eyes, and said, "Yes, I really did take your money, and now I'm trying to return it to you, with interest."

The truth of the matter slammed into me. For a second, there were no words or thoughts available to me as I gasped. Then I stood up so fast that I almost knocked the chair over.

"No, no! I don't believe you! Why? Why would you do that?" My fists were clenched in small balls against my side, and I was trembling all over. "Please say something. Lie to me and tell me you didn't take my money! Anything but that!"

There was no way I could accept his confession—it was too much for me to swallow.

In as even of a voice as he could muster, Dad said, "I was supposed to work for Mr. Miller last Saturday. But he had to go out of town, so I didn't. I had planned on that money, and had figured it into the budget. I didn't have enough grocery money to give your Mother for this week, so I took your savings. I planned to put it back tomorrow—I got paid today. I thought you'd never know the difference."

"Oh, Daddy…"

"I'm sorry I caused you so much trouble and took your money, but there was nothing else I could do."

I just stood there, dumbfounded, feeling somehow cold and hot at the same time. I looked at my father and said quietly, "Oh yes, there was. You could have asked me to borrow the money. I would have gladly given it to you…with no interest charged."

There was nothing left to say, so I just slowly stepped away from him and went upstairs to go back to my room. As I was going up the steps, I heard a scamper of small feet that went from the air return grill into Pat's and my bedroom. She had been listening to the whole conversation, but I didn't even feel irritated with her. In fact, I don't think, at that time, that I *felt* anything but deep sadness. As I passed Jim's door I could tell his light was off, but somehow I knew he was lying in his bed awake. I would apologize to him in the morning. He had known all along and hadn't known how to tell me. Perhaps it was better I found out the way I did.

When I entered my room, Pat was in her bed with the covers up to her neck, but also awake. She watched me intently as I took off my bathrobe and got into bed. I couldn't say anything to her either.

I got into bed, turned my face to the wall, and began to silently cry. No thoughts went through my head; just tears flowed down my cheeks.

To my surprise, I felt my sister sit on the edge of my bed and gently stroke my back. "It will be all right. Please don't cry. Tomorrow will be a lot better than today, you'll see."

Just Close Your Eyes and Click Your Heels…

...as told by Pat

They were, quite simply, the most beautiful things I had ever seen. Centered in the show window of Olie's Shoe Store, lifted on a small stand to distinguish them from the other, ordinary shoes, was a pair of dainty, feminine flats that took my breath away. Made of a muted rose patent leather, they glowed and shimmered from an inner depth under the small spotlight focused on them. These were shoes designed for a princess.

I leaned closer to the window in awe and longing—these were truly ruby slippers, lovingly crafted from the heart of the gem itself and much lovelier than anything Dorothy and Toto had turned up in Oz. My breath clouded the window, obscuring my view. Almost in a trance, I turned and entered the store. I stood hesitantly to the side, unwilling to interrupt the adults in the store as they went about their business. Finally, one of the women clerks noticed me and came over to ask if she could help me. "Yes," I replied a little breathlessly, "those shoes in the window, the rose colored flats? Do they come in a size 4?"

"Why, yes, they do," she answered. "In fact, I think the ones in the window are a size 4. Would you like to try them on?"

I glanced down at my feet, clad in white crew socks and my sensible saddle shoes. "Pinnochio feet," I thought in disgust, "they look just like Pinnochio feet. How can I put *those* shoes on Pinnochio feet?" I looked back up and realized the clerk was waiting for an answer.

"No, not right now," I said. "I have to go home and talk to my Mom first." The clerk nodded in understanding, and turned to another customer. I let myself out of the store and headed for home.

It was two weeks until Christmas, and I had finally found the perfect Christmas gift. All the way home, I pictured myself wearing the rose colored flats, so different from my regular school shoes and the black patent Mary Janes that Mom made me wear to church. Those rose slippers were grown-up shoes, with no baby straps to keep them on your feet. I glanced down at my saddle shoes again and frowned. They were definitely clunky, and I was sure that I could hear each of my footsteps thudding against the frozen ground because my shoes were so big and awful.

At home, I let myself in the back door, raced up the three steps and burst through the door into the dining room. "Mom?" I called, "I'm home. Hey, Mom, where are you? I gotta tell you something."

"Out on the back porch," came Mom's answer, "and quit yelling and charging around like a herd of buffalo. You can *walk* out here and talk to me in a civilized tone of voice."

I shrugged out of my coat, tossed it on a dining room chair, and hurried through the kitchen to the back porch where Mom was working at her sewing machine. I leaned on the sewing table and watched as she ran a seam up a length of what looked like work socks. Temporarily distracted, I asked, "Whatcha making? That looks like socks, but it's too skinny for anyone to get it on anything but a toe."

"I'm making a stuffed toy for your little brother for Christmas. It's going to be a monkey, and this is the tail. Would you like to help me stuff it when I get done?"

"Yeah, sure," I replied—I knew it always paid off to be extra helpful around Christmas time. Remembering my mission, I continued, "But, Mom, I gotta talk to you. I found just what I want for Christmas this year. Just the *exact* thing."

"Now, Patty, we've talked about this before. I know that Carl Nelson is trying to sell his pony, but there is no way we can have a horse around here..."

"It's not the pony," I interrupted. "I was just uptown. You know, I took my library books back? Then I was doing some window-shopping and, Mom, there's this really pretty pair of shoes in Olie's. They come in my size, and I just gotta have them. That's what I want for Christmas this year."

Mom let the sewing machine run to a stop and looked up at me. "A pair of *shoes*?" she asked. Her confusion was understandable. I normally gave little thought to clothing or fashion. I was most comfortable wearing my older brother's hand-me-down jeans, big loose shirts, and tennis shoes. I had no time or patience for feminine frippery such as ruffles and ribbons, and dressing up for church on Sunday morning was a form of torture for me.

"Oh yeah, Mom, they're just beautiful. I'd take real good care of them, and I'd only wear them to church and special places."

"But you have a pair of church shoes, and your school shoes aren't worn out yet."

"I know, but they aren't anything like *these* shoes. Oh, Mom, you gotta see them! They're so beautiful! Will you at least *look* at them?" I pleaded.

"Well, all right," she answered me. "The next time we go uptown you can show them to me. I'm not making any promises other than to look, okay?"

"Okay," I agreed, willing to settle for at least that much of a concession for the time being. "When are you going uptown, next?"

"In a day or two, and you can show them to me then. Now, don't beg and pester me about this. I've got a lot of stuff to do to get ready for Christmas."

Two days later I got my opportunity to show Mom the rose flats. It was snowing, and Mom had picked us up from school. Then we went uptown so she could mail a package to my aunt. After we were done at the Post Office, Mom drove down Main Street and parked the car in front of Olie's Shoe Store. As she turned off the car she said to my brother and sister, "All right, Patty wants to show me something in one of the stores—we'll only be a minute. I need you two to keep an eye on Raymond while we're in the store." Since Raymond was ensconced in his car seat, happily twisting the little plastic steering wheel attached, Donna and Jim glanced at each other and decided that baby-sitting wouldn't be that big of a burden.

I would have skipped up to Olie's window, but I had on my red rubber boots because of the snow. Red rubber boots don't lend themselves to anything but trudging along, so I slogged up to the window with Mom close behind me. I held my breath in fear that the shoes would be gone, but they were still there. With the overcast day and the snow falling around us, the show window glowed all the more brightly. I let out my breath with a sigh and whispered, "There they are. The rose colored ones. Oh, Mom, aren't they gorgeous? That's what I want for Christmas!"

"Well, they are very pretty, and they would certainly look lovely with your Sunday dress. I wonder what they cost? Let's find out." Together, Mom and I went into Olie's. I stopped by the front of the store so I could gaze at the shoes, and Mom went up to one of the clerks and talked for a minute or so.

When she came back, she had a troubled look on her face. "Okay, Patty, let's go. Your brothers and sister are probably getting cold."

When we got outside I asked, "How much are they, Mom? What did the lady say?"

"They're nine dollars, Patty."

My heart sank. Nine dollars! That was a small fortune, and I had never known my mother to pay that much for a pair of shoes. We got in the car and went home; all the way, my mind was churning around that ominous number—*nine dollars*. But, it was Christmas, and I could always hope for some type of Christmas miracle. I just had to have those shoes!

The next afternoon I helped Mom stuff the toy monkey while Raymond took his nap. While we were working, Mom said to me quietly, "Patty, I need to tell you something about those shoes that you want." I held my breath and just nodded my head to let her know I was listening. She continued, "I talked to your Dad about it last night, and I'm afraid that we just can't afford those shoes right now. We've already bought most of the Christmas gifts, and I still have to get the stuff for Christmas dinner. We would love to get them for you, but there's just no room in the budget right now. Maybe they'll go on sale sometime after Christmas, and we can see about it then. Do you understand?"

I could feel the tears prickling the back of my eyelids. I looked down at my hands and centered all of my concentration on pushing stuffing into the monkey arm I was working on. I knew the budget was always tight, and I had watched many times while Dad spent hours wrestling over the figures in his *Headache Book* trying to work out how to cover just basic expenses. I kept pushing stuffing into the various monkey parts until I had control of myself. Then I said, "It's okay, Mom. Thanks for trying, and maybe they *will* go on sale." She just nodded in reply, and we worked quietly for another fifteen minutes, or so, until the monkey was ready to be assembled. Mom thanked me for helping her, picked up the pieces of the toy, and carried them back to the sewing room.

I went up to my room and sat on the end of my bed. Leaning my right arm on the window ledge, I stared out at the darkening landscape and thought about those rose colored shoes—*my* rose colored shoes. How could I get them?

My cash reserves had been reduced to four cents after I had finished my Christmas shopping for the family, and I had only two more allowances coming before Christmas. Dad had increased our allowances so that Jim and Donna (both teenagers) now got fifty cents a week and I got thirty-five cents.

If I subtracted the money for church collection and didn't buy anything else, I would still have only fifty-four cents at Christmas. Report cards were due tomorrow when school closed for Christmas vacation, and I knew my grades would be good enough to net me approximately another dollar, but that would still leave me miles from my goal of nine dollars.

I sighed heavily, leaving a foggy patch on the window. I absently rubbed my forearm across the window, using my sleeve to clear away the fog, and looked out again. The streetlight had come on, and it had begun to snow—you could see the big fat flakes drifting down through the light. Almost in a trance, I watched as the snow added a fresh white patina to everything outdoors. Then it hit me—snow! It was snowing and showed no sign of stopping soon! Maybe I had found the way to get my shoes!

The next day we got out of school early for Christmas vacation. I hurried home and gave Mom my report card, then raced upstairs to change into jeans and a sweatshirt. After a quick lunch of toasted cheese sandwiches and tomato soup, I bundled up for the outdoors, got the snow shovel out of the garage, and headed out to make my fortune. I would shovel sidewalks for fifty cents each, and the shoes would be mine in no time.

When I got to Washington Street, it became apparent that my idea was not unique—the boys in junior high and high school were already out and busily clearing driveways and sidewalks. The pickings were pretty slim. I trudged down the street, stopping at every house with an uncleared walk and inquiring if I could shovel the sidewalk. Most of the ladies who answered the doors told me that their husband or son would be doing it later. In other words: thanks, but no thanks. At about three in the afternoon, I finally got a taker. Mrs. Carlson was an elderly widow who went to our church, and she agreed to let me have a go at her sidewalk.

I dug in and began shoveling as fast as I could. The snow was only a few inches deep, but it was heavy, wet snow. It would be perfect for building snowmen, but it was a major challenge to shovel. My initial burst of energy faded quickly, and the sidewalk seemed to grow longer with each shovelful of snow heaved off to the side. When I finally finished, I had the sidewalk cleaned to the street, and the public sidewalk across the width of the Carlson yard was also clear. It was already dark as I trudged back to the front door and collected my fifty cents—it had taken me almost two hours to clear away all that snow.

It was too late to try for another one, and I knew that I had to get home for dinner. As I made my way home, I was cold, tired and my arms and back ached. I dragged the snow shovel behind me, lacking the energy to carry it the four blocks to our house. As I plodded along, I became more and more depressed. My grand scheme for earning money wasn't working very well, and I figured I would be dead before I managed to shovel nine dollars worth of sidewalks. With the bigger boys also out shoveling, I would be dead before I could even *find* nine dollars worth of sidewalks still available to shovel! In my mind, the rose shoes glimmered as they receded to an unreachable distance.

I made it through dinner, struggling to stay awake. My arms ached and felt so weak that I wondered if I could even lift my fork as far as my mouth. When we finished, Mom and Donna picked up our plates, took them to the kitchen, and returned with dessert. While there was conversation all through dinner, this was the time of day when we sat together as a family and discussed our day while Mom and Dad finished their last cup of coffee. It was also the time of day for "special" things. That night, Dad started by complimenting us on our report cards and handing out the payment for grades—ten cents for each A; five cents for each B; nothing for a C; we owed him five cents for a D; and, God forbid, if you actually ever got an F you owed Dad ten cents for it. As usual though, we had all finished in the money, and Dad was prepared to pay up for our achievements. I got ninety cents. Next, he handed out our weekly allowances—another thirty-five cents for me, but a dime of that had to go into the church collection basket. I had netted a dollar and fifteen cents.

I tucked my money in my pocket, and sat silently while the conversation droned on around me. I was in a half doze when Mom reached out and gently shook my shoulder. "Patty? Patty! What's wrong with you tonight? You've been so quiet and sleepy since you got home—what's going on?" I looked up and saw everyone looking at me expectantly. I sighed heavily and told them about my sidewalk shoveling experience. When I was done, Mom said, "It was a good idea, but that's awfully hard work for a ten-year-old. Maybe there's something else you could do?" I just nodded, but for the life of me I couldn't think of anything else.

Later that night as Donna and I were getting ready for bed, she said to me, "You know, Patty, shoveling sidewalks wasn't a very good idea for making money."

"Oh, thanks!" I snapped back, "So it was a stupid idea; so what? I don't even want to talk about it!"

"Now wait a minute—don't go getting all mad on me. What I was going to say is that you need to think of something else…"

"Like what? Weeding gardens? It's *December*!" I threw myself on my bed and started crying into my pillow. "I'm *never* going to get those shoes," I moaned.

"Well, geez Louise. Will you stop howling? It's not the end of the world! You're smart enough—you just need to figure out something that people need that's easier than shoveling snow. Something they would pay for, and you can't charge too much, so it has to be something you can do quickly. That way, you can do a lot and make your money that way." My sister had just introduced me to the concept of volume merchandising. It was a great concept, but I lacked a product or service to sell. That night, I fell asleep with various moneymaking schemes churning around in my brain.

Overnight, the temperature plummeted to about ten degrees, and we awoke to a world that sparkled and glittered as if diamond dust had been scattered over everything. The wet snow of the day before now had a crust on it that would crunch and squeak under your footsteps. As I looked out my bedroom window, I saw Dad in the driveway. He had an old bucket in his hands, and was scattering ashes from the furnace over the slick, shining surface of the driveway. I grinned as I realized that I had the answer to my dilemma.

After breakfast, I again bundled up for venturing outdoors. I got an old box from the basement, and spent a little time figuring out how to secure it to my sled. We had an old coal-burning furnace, and when Dad cleaned the ashes out of it he put them in an empty fifty-gallon oil drum that he had brought home from the air base. The metal drum was a safe place to store the ashes until they were completely cooled. I filled an old bucket with cold ashes, then hauled them outside and dumped them into the box on my sled. It took several trips to fill the box, and on the last trip up from the basement I also brought along the small gardening spade. After placing the spade into the box, I took off on my rounds.

I got to Washington Street and looked down the rows of cleared sidewalks with satisfaction—it was just as I had thought. Thanks to all those energetic boys, the sidewalks had been cleared the evening before but they had still been wet. This morning, they all had a glaze of treacherous ice. Staying on the snow, I marched up to the front door of the first house and rang the bell. The housewife answered the door, and I immediately began my pitch. "Good morning. I noticed that your sidewalk is pretty icy and slick, and for a dime I'll spread ashes on it."

The woman glanced out at her sidewalk, then looked at me and asked, "Ashes? What kind of ashes?"

"They're furnace ashes, and my Dad says they're the best thing to use. They just wash away later, and they won't hurt your yard or flowerbeds like salt does. He says they're good for the flowers."

"And all you want is a dime?"

"That's right, a dime. Then you won't have to worry about someone falling and getting hurt."

"Well, I guess that is a good idea. Wait just a minute while I get your dime." The woman turned away from the door and picked up her purse from a nearby table. I wanted to hug myself I was so happy. She gave me a dime that I slipped down inside my mitten, and then I set about thoroughly covering her sidewalk with ashes. Within a few minutes, I was on my way to the next house. While it was true that not every householder wanted ashes on their sidewalk, enough of them did that by noon I had run out of ashes. My mitten, however, jingled with its increasingly heavy load of coins. I decided to go home for a short break.

When I got home I ran up to my room, pulled off my mittens, and dumped my accumulation of dimes and a few nickels onto the center of my bed. I spread the coins out and then decided I could count it later—I scooped it all up and put it in my marble bag with my other dollar and sixty nine cents. I still had the rest of the day to earn more. I pulled off my coat and snowpants, and then went and stood on the heat register in the bathroom for a while to warm up.

After lunch I reloaded my box with ashes and took off again. By then, people had been solving their slippery sidewalk problems in other ways, and my customers were farther apart. I kept doggedly on, determined that I wouldn't go home until my box was empty or it got dark. As it turned out, it started getting dark first, but I was so tired from all the walking that I was happy to turn for home. My mitten gave off a very satisfying jingle when I shook it, and the box of ashes was *almost* empty. Towing my sled behind me, I walked through the deepening twilight with a big sense of accomplishment. Surely I had accumulated enough money to buy those shoes!

After dinner I dumped my hoard of coins onto my bedspread and began counting. I had a grand total of five dollars and seventy-nine cents. I had spent the entire day and spread ashes on forty-one sidewalks, but I was still short of my goal. That was a little disappointing, but the fact of earning four dollars and ten cents in one day was exciting. One more day was all I needed.

The next day was Sunday. That meant that the morning was consumed with going to Mass, and with helping Mom at the big family breakfast afterwards. It was one in the afternoon before I could start out again. This day, customers were even scarcer. By four in the afternoon I had netted a lot of rejection, fifty cents, and four lectures about the sin of working on the Sabbath. Cold and disgusted, I decided that it was time to go home.

Over the next few days I wrestled with the problem of how to earn some more money. The weather had warmed up enough to melt most of the snow, so my ash business was temporarily closed. Each night I prayed for sleet, but it didn't materialize. I started pestering Mom for jobs or chores to earn some money. After three days of it, her patience began to wear thin—I was firmly told that I was not to ask again, and if she came up with a job for me she would let me know. My spirits sank again, and I started moping around the house and picking fights with my brother and sister. As a result, I spent a large portion of my daytime hours in the thinking chair.

While I never found out for certain, I suspect that my sister was the one who told Mom what was going on. On the afternoon of December 23rd Mom was in the kitchen baking Cherry Wink cookies for Christmas. She called me in to sample the Cherry Winks, and then asked me about how much money I had earned. I told her that I had six dollars and twenty-nine cents total, with another twenty-five cents coming from my allowance that night. Telling her about it simply reminded me how far I was from my goal of nine dollars, and I started crying with the frustration of it all. Mom looked at me for a moment, then said, "Now stop that, it's almost Christmas. You did a very good job of earning money, and you should be happy about it. I didn't realize you had made so much."

"Yeah, but it's still not enough," I blubbered.

"Maybe you did make enough. I know it's hard to earn money, particularly for someone your age, but you earned enough that I think we can do this—if you will pay half, your Dad and I will pay for the other half and we can get your shoes. What do you think?"

What did I think? I couldn't believe I had heard her correctly! I looked up, sniffling and wiping at my eyes with the backs of my hands, and asked, "R-r-really? Really, truly we can get the shoes?"

Mom hugged me and said, "Yes, really truly we can get the shoes. We'll go this afternoon. Now dry your tears and go upstairs and get your money and your good nylon socks." I hugged her in return, hard, then turned and raced for the stairs with Mom's voice calling after me, "*Walk*, and be sure your feet are *clean*."

The next night, Christmas Eve, I wore my new rose slippers in public for the first time. They made their debut at Midnight Mass, and I was certain that everyone was in awe and envy of my beautiful new shoes. I felt like Cinderella when I wore them, and that feeling never went away. Each time I slipped them on I was thrilled anew. My Christmas miracle had happened.

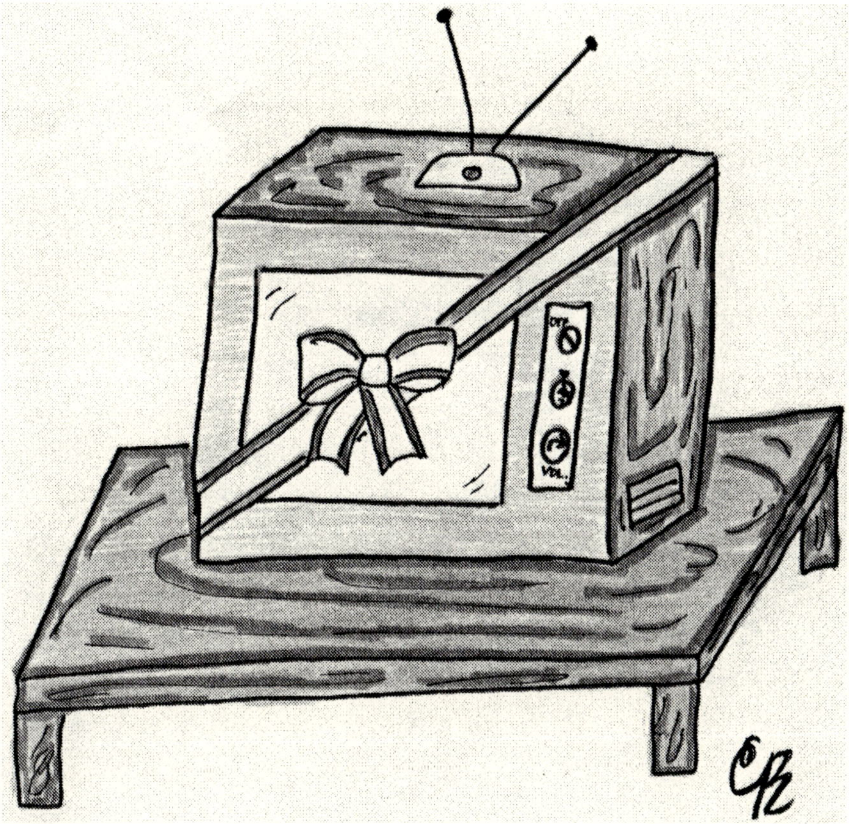

Do You See What I See?

...as told by Donna

I firmly believe that there is a primitive clock inside all children that wakes them up (in unison) early on Christmas morning. My brother, sister and I were no exception to that phenomenon. At exactly 7:00 a.m. our eyes popped open. We were up and out of our beds in a flash, tugging on our bathrobes as we scrambled downstairs to the living room. The Christmas tree lights were on, and there was a treasure trove of presents piled under the tree. Mom and Dad were already up and waiting for us.

All three of us tried to squeeze through the living room door at the same time, as though we had been permanently glued together. My sister was the first to pop out of our squirming little group, with my brother and I tumbling in after her. We all stopped dead in our tracks just inside the room. After several stunned seconds, the silence was broken with one word: "WOW!"

There, sitting on its matching walnut table, with a bright red ribbon and large red bow wrapped around it, was a brand new Zenith television set! We stood motionless, staring in disbelief. The brightly wrapped packages under the tree dulled in comparison, and the bowls of nuts and Christmas candy sitting on the coffee table just feet from our grasp did not temp us to move. We were oblivious to the smells of freshly warmed cinnamon rolls and percolating coffee that drifted into the living room from the kitchen. We had a television set!

"Is it ours? Is it really ours?" my little sister, Patty, asked incredulously.

"Well, I didn't steal it," responded Dad. "Of course it's ours."

"Did we get rich or something?" I asked, still not believing it was real. (About one third of the population of our small town owned television sets, and most of them were members of the "rich folks" group.)

My mother chuckled at my question and said, "No we didn't get rich overnight. We've been saving up for this for many months. Your father believes it will be very educational for you children. I'm not sure I agree with him, but, nevertheless, we are now the proud owners of a TV."

"Can we turn it on?" asked my brother, Jim.

"Not now," Dad decreed. "We are going to be selective about what we watch and when." (Being "selective," when there was only one television channel available in our area, often called for a stretch in the definition of the word.) "Ed Sullivan is having a Christmas special tonight at seven o'clock, and we will turn it on to watch that."

We knew better than to whine or beg when our father set the game rules, so we turned our attention to the gift unwrapping and sampling of all the holiday goodies. At varying times, though, each of us would look over our shoulder to glance at the new television set, just to make sure it was still there.

After all the Christmas day traditions were over and we had stuffed ourselves with a large turkey dinner, the whole family sat quietly together in the living room. Everyone, including my parents, stared at the blank screen of our new TV. Our mother gently cleared her throat and then matter-of-factly said to our father, "It's almost six-thirty, Leonard; maybe you should get the television set ready. The salesman at Sears said we would have to adjust it before we could watch it." All three of us held our breath. What would he say? Would he turn on the TV, or make us wait even longer?

"That's a good idea," Dad replied. "It probably needs to warm up, too."

He was going to turn it on! He was really going to turn it on, right at that minute in time! I could feel the excitement emanating from my brother and sister, and my heart was thumping too fast for me to sit still. "Can I help!" I blurted out and jumped to my feet. "What can I do?"

"Well, you girls can let me know when I have the TV adjusted correctly. Just sit calmly on the couch and tell me when the picture is coming in clearly."

"Jim," he said to my older brother, "You come over here and read the instruction manual to me. It's hard to hold that book while I'm working." (I guess setting up television sets is a "guy thing." Dad had not even entertained the thought of asking my sister or me to read the instruction manual.)

I resignedly returned to my spot on the couch next to my sister, and my brother, in his most official instructor voice, began to read the step-by-step directions to my Dad. "First of all you need to remove the ribbon and bow from around the television," he said.

"That's not in that book!" I interrupted. "And what's wrong with your voice?"

Everyone stopped and turned and looked at my brother. He cast his eyes down and his face started to turn slightly red.

"Donna!" admonished my mother.

"I'm sorry," I said. "I guess I'm just excited. I'll be quiet."

"Thank you," Mom said softly. "Now, let's continue."

Dad removed the red ribbon and bow from the television and tossed them on the coffee table. My little sister quickly snatched them up as they landed. She put the red ribbon around her neck and stuck the red bow on the side of her hair. She leaned back on the couch with a smug smile on her face. I just stared at her. I always knew she was crazy, and now it was obvious that she was a Christmas nut as well!

My brother began again, "Step one: Before supplying power to the unit, remove the back panel by loosening the four screws located on the upper right and left and the lower right and left corners."

"Damn!" my father said. "I need my Phillip's screwdriver. I better go down to the basement and get my tool box."

"Leonard, watch your language!" my mother scolded. "I have a Phillip's screwdriver in my sewing room. You can use it."

Before he could say a word, she was up and out of the living room, on her way to her sewing room. We silently waited for her to return so that Dad could continue getting the new TV ready to watch. When she came back into the room, Mother handed Dad a bright new screwdriver. The yellow handle was still translucent with no greasy fingerprints smudged all over it. Dad looked at the screwdriver and then at my mother in total bewilderment. "But...where..." he began to say.

Mother interrupted him, "It's getting closer to seven o'clock, so let's finish up quickly." After staring at the screwdriver in his hand for a minute, Dad proceeded to remove the back panel on the set.

Jim continued to read through the next steps. What it amounted to was that Dad had to insert four vacuum tubes in the slots labeled A, B, C, and D in the back of the television. He also had to connect some wires together. I didn't understand why he had to do these things, just that the instruction book, via my brother's succinct reading, told him to do so.

When Dad was finished putting the tubes in the set and connecting all the appropriate wires, he sat back on his heels and exclaimed, "Let's plug this beauty in and see if it works!" With electrical cord in hand, he reached for the nearest wall plug.

"Dad, wait!" Jim stopped him in mid reach. "It says here that you have to put the panel back on before you plug it in or you could get electrocuted!"

"I thought I'd leave it off until I was sure the TV would come on. If I connected something wrong, I could fix it without having to take the panel back off again," Dad explained.

"I don't know, Dad, but it says right here in big bold letters not to do that. It also says the manufacturer will not be responsible for accidents that occur when the back panel is off the television."

Mother stepped in. "Leonard, for safety's sake I think it best we do what the instruction book says. We certainly don't want you to be electrocuted."

"What's 'lectrocuted?" my sister asked.

"The electricity jumps right out of the back of the TV and shocks you," my brother explained. "Kind of like what happens to a person in an electric chair. It could kill you."

We were stunned by this information, and looked at my brother in awe. Seeing our attention focused on him, he continued to elaborate. "When someone is electrocuted in the electric chair their eyeballs actually melt and run down their face," he said with authority. "Their blood boils and their brains fry like bacon. Smoke actually comes out of the top of their head."

Mom interrupted him, "I believe we've heard enough to know that it's dangerous."

"Oh yuck! Oh, gross!" I retorted.

"Co-o-o-ol," was all Pat said.

My father had not moved from where he knelt beside the plug. He stared at my brother as though he were a complete stranger. Jim looked back at Dad and said in defense, "It's true; I read it someplace."

Without saying anything, Dad put the cord down, and, with shaking hands, picked up the panel to the back of the television. He carefully screwed it back on, let out a heavy sigh and gingerly picked up the electrical cord. Leaning back on his heels as far away from the plug as he could, and with his head averted to the side, Dad plugged in the cord.

Nothing happened. There was no brilliant flash of light or smell of ozone in the air. Everything was fine and un-disasterous. (I sometimes wonder whether or not I saw a small look of disappointment on my sister's face.) Oh well, it was time to *turn the TV on!*

On the bottom front of the television was a small door that opened downward. Inside was a panel with four little knobs. The knobs were labeled. The first one said HORT, the second VERT, and the other two CONTRAST and ALIGN. We weren't quite sure what these knobs were for, but we were confident that we would find out.

There was a large dial on the upper right hand side of the set. This was the channel selector with numbers from 1 through 8 stenciled on it. When you turned the selector clockwise it made a very distinct CLICK, CLICK, CLICK sound.

On the right side of the TV were two more knobs. These knobs had little arrow indicators on them. The first knob was labeled towards the left side ON and towards the right side OFF. The second knob said VOL with an elongated, curved arrow pointing downwards. Everyone was an authority on these two knobs, and information burst forth.

Dad's slight irritation showed. "Sit down and be quiet. I know what they mean! If you kids don't calm down, I'm not going to turn this television on!"

With that threat hanging in the air, we quickly sat back on the couch, and for the next several minutes not a word was uttered.

With an air of confidence, Dad reached around to the side of the set and turned the ON/OFF knob. The room was totally silent. All of a sudden, there were fairly loud popping, cracking, and hissing sounds coming from our new TV.

"Oh, my," Mother said.

Then the three of us kids began talking all at once. "Is it broke?" "What are those noises?" "Will Dad get 'lectrocuted now?" "What's wrong with it?" "There's no picture!" "Better stand back, Dad."

"*Quiet!*" Dad demanded in a louder than normal voice. "It's just warming up. The new tubes make those sounds the first time they heat up. Will you please be patient?"

We shut up instantly, and zeroed our sights on the black screen. To our amazement a small white dot appeared in the center of the screen. It was like a hypnotist's ploy. This sight was mesmerizing and focused our attention completely. No one moved. The dot slowly grew larger and larger and larger until the entire screen was all white.

We waited with bated breath. Grey lines began to appear, rolling diagonally across the screen. If there was a picture somewhere in those lines, we couldn't discern it. The lines grew darker and fatter as they scrolled sideways. We tried not to say anything, but we all started talking at the same time again.

"Give me a chance to adjust this, will you please," pleaded my Dad. "Jim, will you read me what the instruction manual says to do next?"

"Okay, Dad. Locate the variable capacitor labeled 'Vert. Hold' and rotate to stabilize signal synchronization. After synch. has been established, adjust the High V potentiometer trimming the output of the fly-back transformer…"

Jim stopped reading, and looked at Dad over the top of the manual. Jim's brow was furrowed with confusion. Dad was staring back at him as if he was speaking in tongues. Pat and I shut up too.

Dad said, "All right. 'Vert. Hold' must mean these knobs on the front. Let's try adjusting them." Dad turned back to the four knobs on the panel in the front the TV and began twisting them at random. Sometimes the lines got smaller; sometimes they got bigger. At one point the lines changed direction from left-to-right then right-to-left.

Then the screen went completely black, and we all uttered a disappointed "o-o-o-o-h." Dad glared at us again to command silence. Finally, like magic, we heard sounds and distant voices coming from our new television set. There was a chorus of approval, and we all clapped our hands.

We had sound, but still no picture. Jim, though not sanctioned, spoke up, "I think it might be the rabbit ears, Dad. Maybe they need to be repositioned."

Not wanting to be upstaged, Dad said, "I was just thinking the same thing."

He first checked that the antenna leads were firmly attached to the contacts at the back of the television. Satisfied that they were not loose, he began to move the antenna arms around, pointing them in a variety of directions and positions. The screen came back on all light grey, but now it was covered with a very white snowstorm.

"Maybe they're having a blizzard in New York," Jim commented. Pat and I giggled behind our hands, and received one of those "Mother looks" for our transgression. We quickly stifled our laughter and tried to look very interested in what Dad was doing. Dad said nothing in response to my brother's remark, but instead continued to fiddle with the rabbit ears.

Unnoticed by anyone, Mom had picked up the instruction manual and was reading it quietly. "It says in here that, depending on your location, it might be necessary to create a contact point for one of the antenna arms to get a clearer reception. I wonder what that means?"

"One of the arms needs to touch something," my brother clarified. Dad moved the antenna arm nearest the window so that it was touching the metal frame of the storm window. It worked! A picture started to form. It was jumpy and very blurred, but it was a distinguishable picture.

"I've heard that if you put tin foil on the rabbit ears it works even better," Jim advised.

"Tin foil!" Dad exclaimed.

By the look on his face you could tell there was no way he was going to wrap tin foil anywhere on his new TV. He was appalled by the idea! My God, tin foil was for covering the turkey, not a brand-new television set! Dad looked at my brother again as though he might be seeing an alien for the first time. Or perhaps, for just a moment in space and time, Dad may have been wondering if there was a possibility that this child had been switched at birth.

After a small shake of his head to clear his thoughts, he continued. "Patty, come over here and hold the other antenna arm up as high as you can reach while I try to adjust it some more."

My sister jumped up from the couch and scurried over to the TV. She was noticeably proud that she had been chosen for this most important task. After she took her position I thought she looked like a miniature Statue of Liberty standing there with her arm held up in the air holding the antenna like a torch. I rolled my eyes at her and was about to point this similarity out when the voice *and face* of Ed Sullivan came from the TV.

We were ecstatic! By today's standards, it was a far cry from a good picture. We didn't care. It was working! There, right in the middle of our living room, we were watching a show that came all the way from New York City! This was indeed the entertainment wonder of all times!

Dad, looking quite pleased with himself, stood up and went and sat in his favorite chair. Mom put down the instruction manual, and focused her attention on Ed Sullivan, who was introducing an acrobatic troop from Spain. Jim and I sat as far forward as we could on the couch so that we would not miss one second of viewing. We were all engrossed, and deeply happy.

Our concentration, though, was interrupted by a pitiful, little voice coming from the corner of the room near the TV. "Do I have to stand here all night and hold this antenna?"

O Tannenbaum

...as told by Pat

"Well, I'm planning to take down the Christmas tree tomorrow," said Mom. "Who would like to help me with that?"

All of us immediately volunteered to participate in this annual tradition that officially closed the Christmas season. It was Friday night of the second week in January. Christmas and New Year's Day had come and gone, followed by the Feast of the Epiphany on January 6th. We had added the wise men and camels to the manger set on that day, closing that story for another year. The Christmas tree was the only thing left to be taken care of.

We always had a live tree for Christmas, and we put it up during the weekend before Christmas. Mom told us that the 12 days of Christmas were the days from December 25th until January 6th, so our tree remained up and decorated for that entire time. The first weekend after the 6th was the appointed time for the tree to come down.

Noting that she had a full complement of volunteers for the task, Mom added, "All right, we'll start getting things ready after we've cleaned up the dinner things. First thing tomorrow, we'll start taking it down."

We were up early the next morning, eager to begin on the tree. Over breakfast we chattered happily about what a nice Christmas it had been, and the other things we planned to do that weekend after the tree was down. Outside, a light snow was lazily sifting down from a gray sky. When we were finished, Mom said, "Okay, everyone take their dishes out to the kitchen, and let's clear the table. The washing up can wait until after we're done with the tree." The table was cleared so fast that it might have been magic.

We gathered in the front room and began removing the decorations from the tree. Mom had the ornament boxes laid out, and there were stacks of fresh tissue paper at hand. We would take an ornament from the tree, remove the hook, and then carefully wrap each bauble in tissue before tucking it away in a box. Jim, being the tallest, collected the ornaments from the top of the tree, I got the ones from the middle, and Raymond and Donna were acting as a team clearing the lower branches. Ray was now 3 years old and was allowed to help with the tree. Mom had explained to him that the ornaments could break very easily, so he would have to be careful. He would collect an ornament, and then, handling it as gently as if it were a soap bubble, he would cautiously take it to Donna. Under Ray's watchful gaze, she would wrap it and put it away in a box. Satisfied that everything had been handled properly, he would return for another one.

After the ornaments were all removed, Mom produced a paper grocery sack to be used as a trash bag, and we began removing the tinsel. Mom reminded us that it was important to get every strand of tinsel from the tree. Finally, the only things left on the tree were the lights and the angel at the top. Jim lifted the angel from her perch, and Mom slipped her into her box filled with crushed tissue. Then, while Jim removed the strands of lights, Ray and I packed up the manger scene, wrapping each figurine and packing them all into the stable now lying on its back.

Finally, it was all done. The tree stood as it had when it first entered our home, now looking a little forlorn stripped of all its decorations. The boxes of ornaments, lights, and the manger were neatly stacked along the wall, ready to be put away for another year. Mom surveyed the scene, making sure that the tree was absolutely bare, with every decoration and every scrap of tinsel gone. She nodded and said, "Excellent. You've done a perfect job." Then she turned to us with a big smile and sparkling eyes and asked, "Now, is everyone ready to put it up again?"

"You bet!"

"Yes! Let's do it!"

"I'll go tell Dad. I think he's down in the basement."

Still smiling, Mom added, "Patty, after you tell Dad we're ready, bring up one of the tree baskets with you. Okay? And, Jim, why don't you go down with her and bring up the rest of the things?"

"I'll get the box of stuff from the kitchen," added Donna.

I ran for the basement stairs and raced down them as fast as I could, calling as I went, "Dad! Hey, Dad! We're ready to put the tree back up." Jim was right behind me.

"Okay," Dad answered, "Everything's ready outside so I'll be right up."

A few minutes later we were all in the front room again, watching as Dad and Jim removed the Christmas tree from its stand and laid it on a sheet that Mom had spread on the floor. Pulling the edges of the sheet up and around the tree (to catch and contain loose needles) they carried the tree to the back door and outside, where they laid it gently in the driveway. They came back in, and we all bundled up for the outdoors with coats, hats, scarves, gloves and boots.

Outside once again, we made a small parade as we tramped across the back yard to the far end of the garden. Dad was in the lead, carrying the Christmas tree, and we followed behind, each of us carrying a loaded basket or box. Even Raymond was carrying a brown paper bag with the top folded down.

While we had been removing the tree decorations, Dad had sharpened a tall stake and driven it into the ground at the back edge of the garden. Carefully, he and Jim lifted the Christmas tree against the stake and securely wired the trunk of the tree to it. Now it was time to decorate the tree once more.

The night before, after dinner, we had spent some time preparing things for the tree. Using fine wire, we had strung popcorn and cranberries into long ropes. There were hard biscuits that were coated with peanut butter and rolled in birdseed, and about a half dozen apples that we had wrapped wire around to make "cages" to contain the fruit. The baskets from the basement held dried ears of corn and sunflower heads dense with seeds. These were the new decorations for the tree.

We worked hard, wiring the various goodies to the branches of the tree. We picked out a particularly large sunflower head that Dad and Jim fastened to the top of the tree like a star. When the branches were loaded, we looped the ropes of popcorn and cranberries around the tree. As a final touch, we opened Raymond's bag, which contained pumpkinseeds from our Halloween jack-o-lanterns. Mom had dried and saved them. We scattered the creamy white seeds among the branches and under the tree. When we were done, we stepped back to admire our handiwork.

Our Christmas tree stood proudly with its branches filled once more. The light snow was still falling, and the sparkling flakes caught in the dark green boughs. Mom gazed at it in satisfaction and said, "Now, the birds and small animals can have a Christmas, too. And, we'll refill it as it's needed, because it's hard for them to find food in the winter. Okay, let's take this stuff back up to the house."

We each picked up a basket, bag, or box and carried them back to the house. The baskets still had lots of corn and sunflowers, and we had only used about a third of the pumpkinseeds. As Mom had said, those supplies would be used to refill the tree when needed.

Our Christmas tree stood at the edge of the garden for the rest of the winter, providing a handy smorgasbord for the local wildlife. We had a clear view of it from the window of our back porch, and we often saw the scarlet flash of cardinals and the bright turquoise of blue jays as they visited the tree. Fat pheasants would come, too, waddling around the bottom of the tree as they feasted. After a fresh snowfall we would take a small guidebook out and try to identify the tracks of animals that had visited. We found the tracks of raccoons, rabbits, squirrels, and opossums. Occasionally we would find the neat, cloven tracks of deer.

As the winter passed, our tree became more and more bedraggled as it withstood the storms and the activity of the birds and animals. By spring it was little more than a skeleton with a circular carpet of pine needles, twigs, and seed hulls beneath it. Our supplies of corn and sunflowers were finally exhausted, but, with the warming weather, other food sources were becoming available for the wildlife. Still, we didn't take down our Christmas tree because it had one more job to do.

*   *   *

On a warm day in early spring I hurried home from school, bursting with my news. Mom was outside, raking out one of the flowerbeds where tender green shoots of tulips and narcissus were poking from the ground.

"Hey, Mom, guess what I saw today? The first robin!"

"Oh, that's nice. I've seen one or two of them today, myself, and I've heard a few more. I guess that makes it officially spring."

"Right! And it means we have to fix the Christmas tree again."

"That's right, we will. Why don't we plan to do it this weekend? I'm sure it will tickle Raymond to help."

"Okay! Let's do it tomorrow morning!"

Saturday morning I was up early and hurried through my breakfast. After I finished eating I went down to the basement and collected an empty bushel basket. Then I headed next door to the Nelson's. I climbed their back steps and knocked on the door, then stood shifting from foot to foot impatiently while I waited for an answer. In less than a minute, Mrs. Nelson opened the door.

"Oh, good morning, Patty. Do you need something?"

"Yeah. Is Mr. Nelson home today?"

"Ya, but Carl is down in the fields. Is it something I can get for you?"

"Um-m-m, maybe. I need to get a basket of straw."

"And are you going to spin it into gold, like in the Rumpelstiltskin story?"

"No, I need it because we saw the first robins yesterday."

"Ah! So this is something you need for your mama's bird tree, maybe?"

"Yeah, and Mr. Nelson usually gives me a basket of straw."

"Vell, I can get that for you, and I've got something else for you, too. You vait right here, ya, and I'll be back." She left the door and went back into the house while I entertained hopes that the "something else" might be some of her wonderful Swedish butter cookies.

Instead, she returned carrying a small bag that she handed to me. I peeked inside and found it filled with snippets of string and puffs of cotton batting that had been saved from the tops of pill bottles. She smiled at me and said, "I think the birds can use that, too, don't you? Let's go get the straw."

We walked down to the barn together, where we filled the basket with fresh, clean straw. When it was full, I tucked the bag on top and said, "Thanks a lot, Mrs. Nelson. This is just what we needed."

"Oh, ya, and you're velcome. Come and see me again, soon."

I picked up the basket and started for home, and then remembered that Mom always said kindness should be repaid with kindness. I stopped and turned back, asking, "Um-m-m, do you need any help with anything, Mrs. Nelson? Like collecting eggs or something?"

"No, and thank you. I got the eggs earlier. You just go on home and help your mama vith the tree, ya?"

"Okay! Thanks, again!" I turned and hurried home with my supplies.

At home, Mom, Raymond and I carried the basket out to the Christmas tree. Mom had also added a bag of string and cotton tufts to our supplies. We tucked handfuls of straw among the branches, and draped pieces of string on the tree like tinsel. We pulled apart the tufts of cotton batting and snagged it onto twigs all over the tree. When we were done, we had transformed the smorgasbord into a handy building supplies center for the nesting birds.

For the next few weeks, our Christmas tree was once again aflutter with birds. Gradually, the straw and other supplies disappeared, and we were satisfied that *our* birds had the sturdiest and most softly lined nests in town. Finally, it was time to get the garden ready for that year.

The day before Mr. Anderson came out to plow our garden with his small tractor, Dad took down the Christmas tree. He cut it into a couple of pieces and added it to the detritus from the spring raking that had been piled in the middle of the garden. We had a small bonfire that blazed brilliantly as the pine was consumed. After the fire settled to a bed of coals and small flames fed by the winter-dead branches and twigs from the other trees, Mom let us toast marshmallows over it. The next day, the ashes were plowed into the garden.

No one was sad or unhappy that the Christmas tree ended its days like that. It had done its job admirably well, providing happiness for us and for numerous other creatures as it extended the Christmas spirit from the depths of winter through to the promise of a new spring.

Now, Donna and I still get a live tree each year, but we put it up much earlier in December. If we wait until the weekend before Christmas, we find that the pickings are pretty thin at the tree lots. The tree has to come down earlier, also, in order to meet the trash pickup schedule of the Sanitation Department. We take the tree down on New Year's Day, and then I drag it outside to the area by the curb designated for "used Christmas trees." The trees are shredded and ground for mulch. I come back in and get the bag of nutritionally balanced, scientifically sorted, cleaned and mixed birdseed with the resealable top for freshness. I use that to refill the small bird feeder hung in the corner of our patio.

Somehow, it just isn't the same.

The Red Coat

...as told by Donna

Financially, it had been a fairly generous year for my parents. My father had worked for Mr. Miller just about every Saturday since the first of September. This part-time job supplied him with that extra cash everyone needs for those expenses that occur outside of the monthly budget. That year, though, he had worked often enough to have excess money (a rare thing in our family). Mom and Dad decided that this was an opportunity to get all of us kids new winter coats before Christmas. I was thirteen years old.

I tenaciously shopped every store that carried women's coats; I was determined not to settle for anything less than the perfect coat. Eight days before Christmas I found it! The coat was tucked in a rack with about fifty other coats at Laybourn's Fine Ladies Apparel Shop. It was a beautiful coat, and it was cherry red! I had never owned such an elegant, daring and vibrant piece of clothing. The coat was made of the softest wool material imaginable. It was full length, tailor-cut and very grown-up looking. I imagined that it had been made for no one else but me, and that it held a special meaning that was yet to be revealed.

Laybourn's was the upper class women's clothing store in town. We seldom shopped there because the prices were a little beyond our budget. The coat cost a little more than my allotted part of the new coat budget. So, I waited, and continued to shop around. After shopping for several more days, I could not find anything that even came close to the red coat. Every chance I got, I checked in Laybourn's store to make sure no one else had bought it. In fact, I confess that I poked the coat back and behind a post that was in front of the long coat rack, making it hard to see it at first glance. I couldn't stand the wanting. I had to have that coat! I approached Mom and Dad with a deal—if they would agree to buy it, I would agree that the coat would be my big Christmas gift as well. I got the coat, and consented not to wear it until Christmas Eve.

*   *   *

Every year the entire family went to Midnight Mass. It was the tradition that officially meant that Christmas had arrived. I had taken extra care getting ready, applying my minimal makeup as expertly as I could and re-doing my hair twice. I felt very pretty and, surprisingly, very grown up. My new red coat, of course, was my crowning glory. Everything pointed to a very special evening.

When we went outside to get in the car to go to church, we were all stunned. Sometime between dinner and 11:30 p.m. the world had changed. Everything was covered with new snow. There was no visible grass on the lawn and the driveway had disappeared. The snow glistened in the clear moonlight, and it was so white that it almost looked blue. The world had turned to crystal before our eyes. When I looked up, the sky was clear and littered with twinkling stars. The smell in the air was unbelievably clean and crisp. It was a most magnificent display! God had dressed the world in its finest Christmas attire.

The entire family just stood there outside the house gazing at the scene around us. No one made a sound (not even my three-year-old baby brother), and no one moved. Minutes ticked by as the sight before us gradually imprinted its splendor in our minds. *It was Christmas, and this was the most beautiful Christmas Eve we had ever seen!*

Mom was the first to speak, "I guess we better get going or we will be late for church," she said.

I stepped out ahead of the rest of my family to go around to the far side of the car and get into the back seat. I walked behind the trunk of the car, and stayed several feet away so as not to cut through the exhaust. I was alone on the snow-covered driveway. I heard my Mother say, "Oh, my. Donna, stop!" I stopped, turned and looked at her. She paused for a minute, and then to my surprise she said, "Look how beautiful you are tonight in your new red coat framed against the white snow. You look like a Christmas angel with your blond hair as your halo." To my utter surprise I saw the same look in my Mother's eyes that I saw when she first beheld the winter wonderland around us. The rest of my family stood where they were, and nodded their heads in agreement as they looked at me.

I smiled and quietly said, "Merry Christmas, everyone." Dad, Jim, and Pat all responded with a "Merry Christmas," but it was my mother's voice I heard the clearest. "Merry Christmas, Sweetheart," she replied.

I loved that red coat, and wore it until I could no longer squeeze into it.

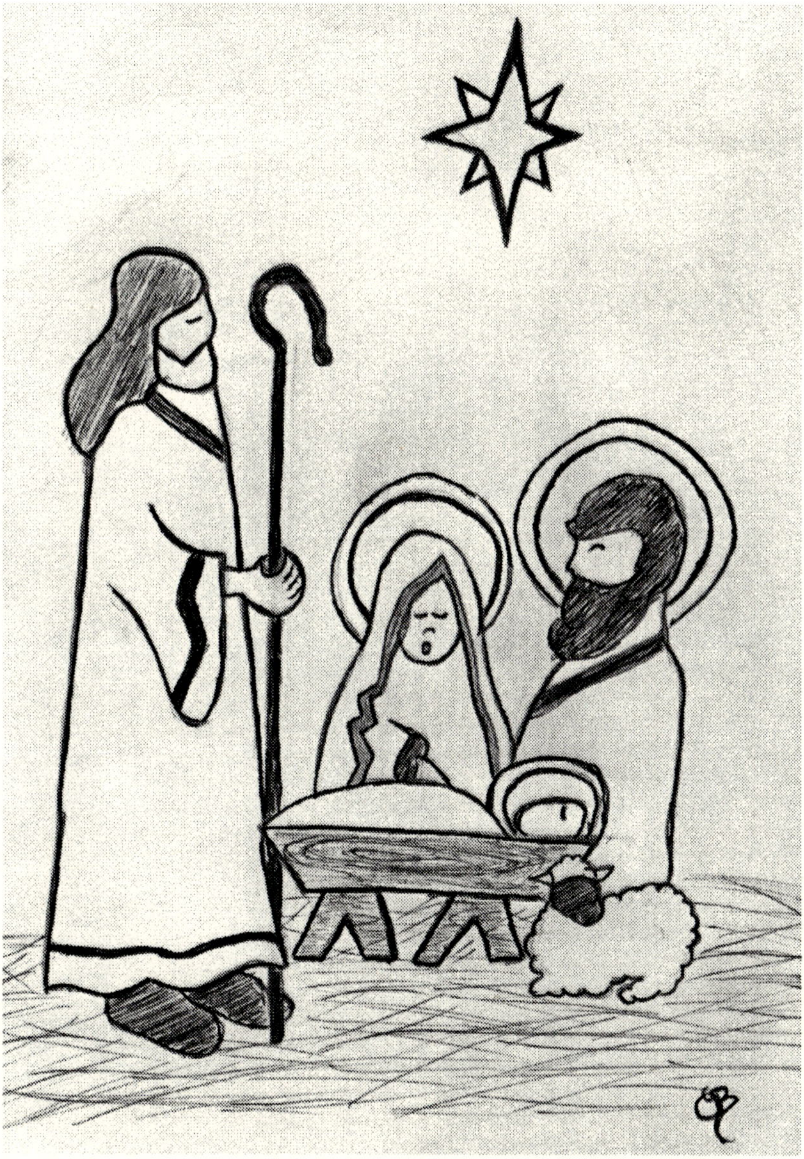

Away From the Manger

...as told by Pat

Jesus was missing! I sat back on my heels in shock, and then leaned forward to look again. It was true. He was simply gone. I was ten years old, and never before within my memory had Jesus ever gone AWOL. The situation was so new and unexpected that I had to think for a minute or so to decide what to do next.

It was the day after Christmas and I was helping Mom by vacuuming the living room carpet. Since I was dealing with the usual post-Christmas detritus of pine needles, glitter, bits and pieces of nutshells and tinsel, I had decided to use the upholstery attachment on the vacuum and do the carpet on my hands and knees. It took longer, but was far more effective in getting everything out of the pile of the carpet. I had worked my way across the living room floor and was preparing to vacuum under the television when I noticed that the baby Jesus was missing from the manger set.

The manger set had occupied various places in the house, but, once we got our television, the manger always went in the open space under the TV table. The set had a wooden, "shadow-box" style of stable, and painted ceramic figures. Each year Mom used it to illustrate the Christmas story for us, and she spread the story over the entire Christmas season. First, the stable was set up with only an ox and the manger full of hay. About a week before Christmas, Mom would tell the story about Mary and Joseph having to go to Bethlehem for the census. At that point, the figures of Mary, Joseph and the donkey were added to the stable. After Midnight Mass on Christmas Eve, the baby Jesus was placed in the manger and the angel, shepherds and sheep were added. Finally, on the Feast of the Epiphany (January 6th) the wise men and camels were added to complete the story.

As usual, the infant Jesus had been added to the scene after Midnight Mass, and he had happily resided there all day on Christmas. For the life of me, I couldn't figure out why he wasn't still there on the day *after* Christmas. Obviously, there was only one thing to do. I turned off the vacuum cleaner and went in search of my mother to tell her about it, and to issue an APB on the missing child.

I found Mom upstairs in the bathroom, straightening the linen closet and putting away the clean folded linens. I marched into the middle of the room, placed my hands on my hips, and announced, "Jesus is gone!"

Mom continued stacking towels and sheets as she calmly replied, "Oh, sweetheart, he's not gone. I know that sometimes it feels like he is, but Jesus is always there for you. What happened to make you feel like this?"

"That's not what I meant! What I *meant* was *Jesus* is *missing!*"

Mom turned and looked at me carefully for a second. Then she said, "This might work better if you start at the beginning and tell me what happened. Okay?"

I huffed in exasperation. "Well, I was vacuuming the living room, and I got over by the TV, and someone stole the baby Jesus out of the manger set. I looked all around and he's nowhere. Somebody stole him."

"Are you sure he didn't just get moved a little? Raymond has been very interested in the manger this year. And, you know how he picks up pieces to look at them. Maybe he just put it back down over to the side."

"Nope. I looked *everywhere* under the TV, and Jesus is just plain *gone*. I bet Raymond did take it, and I bet he *broke* it!"

"Now, Patty, that's not fair and you know it. You're making wild accusations without any basis at all. I'm sure the baby Jesus will show up somewhere. Now, you run along and find something to do."

I turned and stomped out of the room, thoroughly frustrated by what appeared to me as Mom's cavalier attitude about the whole thing. I preferred life to be orderly, and in an orderly world baby Jesus did not simply disappear from the Christmas manger scene, particularly not *after* Christmas. Convinced that my two-year-old brother had taken the statuette and broken it, I decided to hunt out the incriminating evidence. I spent the rest of the afternoon lifting cushions on furniture, peering under beds, sorting through my brother's toy box, and generally searching every hiding place that I knew of in the house. Jesus remained obstinately lost.

At the end of dinner that night Mom brought up the subject of the missing baby Jesus. She quietly mentioned that I had found the piece to be missing, and it would be nice if whoever had the statuette would simply return it to the manger set. I thought the news could have used a little more fanfare, coupled with dire threats to the offender, but I knew better than to say anything about that.

The next morning, Jesus was back in the manger with his quiet little smile firmly in place and his arms opened wide to embrace the world. He definitely wasn't giving out any information as to where he had spent the night.

Over the next several days, the baby Jesus would disappear and reappear with a maddening inconsistency. I began checking the manger set every time I was in the living room. Since I would kneel down on the floor to do my checking, Mom suggested that I take advantage of the position and say a little prayer each time.

My older brother Jim suggested that we make a flip sign and hang it under the TV—in large letters we could have "**Jesus is *IN***" on one side and "**Jesus is *OUT***" on the other. Then we could just flip the sign to the appropriate situation and be able to check the "Jesus status" at a glance. All in all, it seemed that no one in the family was taking the situation seriously.

The mystery finally resolved itself on New Year's Eve. Over dessert after dinner Mom said, "Well, I finally found out where the baby Jesus has been going." We all looked up with interest as she continued, "I was changing the sheets on Raymond's crib today, and I found the baby Jesus tucked in under his blanket. When I asked him why he took it, he told me that he thought Jesus would get awfully cold in that manger. He wanted the baby to be warm and comfortable. If you think about it, it makes a lot of sense—the baby Jesus is wearing only that little scrap of cloth that's rather like a diaper, while everyone else in the stable is pretty well bundled up. So, I told Raymond that as long as he was careful, he could share his crib with the baby Jesus anytime he wanted to. Also, while the baby is in the manger we're going to add this." She held up a small piece of blue flannel that had been cut to the shape of a manger-sized blanket and edged with satin ribbon.

I found myself feeling ashamed of the mean things I had thought about my little brother. Only two years old, he saw the manger scene as a living story, and he had the compassion to feel sorry for the poor little baby.

For the rest of that holiday season, Jesus spent many comfy hours tucked up in Raymond's crib. The little flannel blanket became a standard piece of our manger set—every year when the infant Jesus was added to the manger after Midnight Mass, he was carefully tucked in with his own blue blanket to protect him from the cold.

The Holly and the Tin Foil?

...as told by Pat

It was Saturday, about two weeks before Christmas, 1962, and Dad had a secret. A few days before, he had arrived home with a large box, which he whisked down into the basement and hid. Since then, he had been hugging the secret to himself, and almost fizzing with the excitement of it.

We figured that he had shared the secret with Mom, but there was no hope of prying it out of her. She could be tighter than a clam when it came to secrets, and besides, she was focused on the fact that Jim would be coming home from college for Christmas break. He was coming via Greyhound, and was due in that very afternoon.

We were finishing up breakfast when Dad made his "announcement."

"Well, I have a few errands to do uptown this morning. Then, when I get home, I'm going to be working on something on the front porch. I don't want anyone disturbing me or coming out there until I'm done."

"Okay," we agreed.

"When you clean this morning, do the front porch first so that it's ready, and you won't have an excuse to bug me or come out there."

"Sure, Dad," replied Donna. "We'll clean up the breakfast things and then get right to the cleaning."

"Good. Now, your brother is coming home this afternoon, and Mother tells me that you two are going to pick him up. Is that right?"

"That's right. Mom said we could take the car this afternoon and go get him."

"And you know when he's getting in, and where to pick him up?"

"Yup. The bus gets in at 3:30, and it stops up on Pells Street, next to the Rexall."

"Good. Then, let's get the house cleaned up and everything ready, and try not to disturb your mother. She wants to be rested when Jim gets home, and she said we would decorate the Christmas tree later today after he gets here."

Mom worked the graveyard shift as a nurse at the Knights Templar Home, a retirement home for the elderly that was located a few blocks from our house. She got off work at 7:00 in the morning, and the rest of the morning was reserved for her to get some sleep. On weekends, Donna and I were responsible for cleaning the house and keeping an eye on our six-year-old brother, Raymond, while Mom rested. We were used to the drill, but Dad liked to make sure he had all his ducks in a row and that everything was on schedule.

Dad finished his coffee, announced that he would be back in an hour or so, and left the house.

Working together, Donna and I quickly cleaned up the breakfast dishes and set the kitchen to order. Then, as instructed, we began the house cleaning with the front porch. Dad had enclosed it several years before, and it was now an extension of the front room. We always put the Christmas tree there so it could be seen through the wide expanse of the front windows.

While we were working, we chatted back and forth, musing about what Dad's surprise could be.

"So, what do you think Dad's big surprise is?" I asked.

"Oh, who knows? Maybe he found some kind of funky new lights that spell out 'Merry Christmas' or something. You know how he is."

"Yeah, or maybe new ornaments that change colors."

"Well, whatever it is, it'll be some kind of electronic gadget that he can fiddle with all season. He just loves that kind of thing."

"As long as he doesn't short it out and burn up the Christmas tree, I guess it can't be all that bad." We both giggled at the thought, remembering other instances of Dad and his gadgetry.

We enlisted Raymond's aid by giving him the chore of dusting while Donna and I vacuumed, swept, and mopped. We had progressed through the living room and into the dining room with our cleaning before Dad got back home. He came in with a burst of cold air, humming "Jingle Bells" to himself. He slipped out of his coat and boots, and then went down to the basement. He returned carrying his mystery box and some tools, and went straight to the front porch, where he closed the connecting door to the living room.

We had assumed that one of his errands that morning was to get the Christmas tree, but he didn't mention it and there was no sign of a tree. I went to the living room window and looked out at the car and driveway. There was no tree tied to the roof of the car or leaning against the house, waiting to be carried in. I scanned the entire area visible through the window. There was no hint of anything deep green and conical to be seen anywhere. I turned back to Donna and shrugged my shoulders expressively—how could he have *forgotten* to get the Christmas tree?

We continued with the cleaning while Dad remained secluded with his "surprise." There were occasional thumps and bumps from the front porch, punctuated now and again with mild curses, but the door remained firmly closed.

We had finished the cleaning and were putting away the vacuum and cleaning supplies when Dad finally emerged from the porch. "Hey, kids, come here. You gotta see this," he announced.

The three of us trooped into the living room where Dad was standing by the door to the porch. He stepped into the porch, spread his arms wide, and said, "Ta-daa!"

We followed him through the door and stopped dead in our tracks. There was silence for a few seconds, and then Donna asked, "Is that our Christmas tree?" She sounded doubtful.

"You betcha," replied Dad. "It's the newest thing. It doesn't drop needles all over the place, it doesn't dry out and turn into a fire hazard, and we can use it over and over again so it saves a lot of money in the long run. What do you guys think?"

Standing in the place of honor, centered in front of the windows, was the strangest looking "tree" that any of us had ever seen. I could think of nothing to say, and Raymond appeared to have been struck dumb. Donna came to the rescue by saying, "Wow, Dad, I've never seen anything like this. It sure is shiny."

Dad gazed lovingly at his new acquisition. "It sure is," he said proudly. "It's just *beautiful!*" Then he turned back to us. "Well, it's almost time for you girls to go and get Jim, isn't it? I'll just get this box and stuff out of here." He picked up the large box, some packing material, and his tools and carried it all off to the basement.

The three of us were left standing there with the tree. It was an aluminum foil sculpture. The base was a silver colored block into which the trunk had been inserted. The trunk was a six-foot tall, foil-wrapped pole. Spiraling up the trunk at exact intervals were clamps that supported the branches. The effect was that of a silvery broomstick bristling with silvery spines, each one arrow-straight and pointing slightly upward. Each branch was covered with fringed foil, and ended in an odd little foil rosette at the tip. It might have been an alien porcupine and, frankly, it looked like it could inflict some serious injury if someone were to accidentally bump into it.

Raymond tugged on Donna's hand and asked, "What happened, Donna? Can't we afford a real tree this year?"

"No, Raymie," she replied, "Dad wanted something different this year. I guess *this* is our Christmas tree."

"Well, he got *different*, all right," I muttered.

"But," continued Raymond, "Aren't Christmas trees supposed to be green?"

"Well, most of them are green, but I guess they can come in silver, too."

I snorted in disbelief. "Do you think Mom *really* knows what this looks like?"

"That has to be the ugliest thing I have ever seen," said Donna.

"It looks like something out of a grade-B science fiction movie," I replied.

"If it had legs, it could *star* in its *own* science fiction movie!"

In a small voice, Raymond added, "I don't think I like this tree very much."

"Well, don't say anything to Dad about it," cautioned Donna. Then, to distract him, she added, "Pat and I are going to go uptown to get Jim. Do you want to come with us?"

"Can I?"

"Sure. Go put on your coat and stuff, and we'll go." Ray ran off to collect his outdoor gear, and Donna and I looked at each other with consternation in our eyes.

"What can we do about it?"

"Well, maybe we can talk to Mom about it later."

"Yeah, I guess so. Let's go get our coats."

* * *

The Greyhound system was running efficiently that day, and the bus was right on time. Through the windows of the bus, we could see Jim making his way up the aisle, and we started waving the moment his tall, lanky frame appeared in the door. He came down the steps, followed by the bus driver who went to the side of the bus and opened the luggage bay.

Raymond found the luggage bay to be the most interesting thing, so far, and he edged forward to examine it while Jim retrieved his suitcase and duffel bag. Fascinated, Ray had edged so close that he was almost inside the luggage bay, pointing things out and asking what they were. The bus driver, however, was a man on a schedule and didn't have time for a first-grader's questions. He shooed Ray back, closed the cavernous compartment, and climbed back into the bus. The bus pulled away in a cloud of exhaust.

On the way home, Donna and I peppered Jim with questions about college. We wanted to know if his classes were harder than they were last year, had he made new friends, did he still like living in a dorm, and was his new roommate cute as well as smart? Ray just wanted to know how cold it was in Minnesota. In no time at all, we were pulling into the driveway.

Jim retrieved his luggage from the trunk, and all four of us went up the front steps and in through the front door of the house, which put us in the front porch. Jim stopped in his tracks and said, "Mother of Mercy, what is *that?*"

"What?" I replied brightly. "You aren't referring to our new Christmas tree, are you?"

"This is a joke, right? You guys aren't serious, are you?"

"Serious as a heart attack," replied Donna. "That's our new, ultra-modern Christmas tree that doesn't drop needles, catch fire, or need to be thrown out. We get to use it for *years*."

Jim glanced at the two of us and then asked, "Dad, right?"

"Right," we chorused.

"Does Mom know about this?"

"We're not sure, yet."

Ray, quiet until then, now asked, "Jim, aren't Christmas trees supposed to be green? Do they teach you that in college?"

"Well, Raymie, they haven't covered that yet, but I think..."

He was interrupted by Mom's voice, "Is that Jim? Are you home?" She was on her way through the living room, and appeared at the door to the porch seconds later. "Oh, you *are* home. I knew I heard your voice. How are you?" She moved forward and enfolded him in a tight, maternal hug. She let go and stepped back, scanning him critically from head to foot. "You've lost some weight. Are you getting enough to eat?"

"Yeah, Mom, I'm fine."

"Of course you are. And why are we standing around out here?"

"We were just admiring the Christmas tree."

Mom glanced at the tree, and her eyebrows twitched. She turned back to Jim. "Well, you must be cold. Are you hungry? Come into the dining room and we'll have a little something while you tell us about what you've been doing. Then, a bit later, we'll decorate the tree." She led the way to the dining room.

*   *   *

Fueled by a full pot of coffee, the visiting around the dining room table continued until dinner, and throughout the meal. Jim had several entertaining stories about college life, and he showed an admirable interest in the doings of the family and town while he had been gone. After dessert and coffee, Dad said, "Well, I think it's about time to decorate the tree. What do you think?"

We all agreed happily, and trooped out to the front porch. Mom and Dad followed shortly, carrying the boxes of ornaments and lights. They spread the boxes out and began opening them.

I picked up a string of lights and turned to the tree. I started at the bottom, draping the lights from branch to branch. They looked awful—at the least motion they slid down the branch to rest against the trunk, and the dark green electric cord looked like a skinny python looped against all the silver. I quickly stopped, and then ventured a question, "Um-m-m, Dad? How do you put the lights on this, and how do you hide the cord?"

Dad spun around and said, "No! No lights on this kind of tree. Take that off of there. Just put the ornaments on it."

"No lights? Why not?"

Dad's answer was clear enough, "Shock hazard. You could get electrocuted."

I jumped back and eyed the tree warily. A Christmas tree that electrocuted people? What next? Reassuring myself that nothing was plugged in yet, I stepped back to the tree and gingerly removed the string of lights.

Donna had found the box of hooks and had opened several boxes of ornaments while I had been fiddling with the lights. Now she said, "Okay, let's start with the ornaments.

We began hanging ornaments on the silvery, skeletal structure that was going to be our Christmas tree. It didn't take long—there weren't a lot of choices as to where to hang things. There was none of the usual searching for just the right spot where an ornament would hang freely, reflect the sparkle of a nearby light, or perfectly fill in an empty spot.

After the ornaments were hung, Dad said to Mom, "Okay, Bernice, give me the angel and I'll put it on the top."

Mom picked up the box that was used to store the angel, opened it, and carefully began unwrapping and removing the cushioning tissue paper. Our Christmas angel was handmade—years before, Mom had purchased a small, porcelain doll. She had used white satin to create a gown and wings for the doll, and had used clippings from Donna's baby hair to give the angel a coiffure of softly curled, pale blonde hair. The dress and wings could be removed for cleaning when needed, and that beautiful Christmas angel was one of our most enduring Christmas traditions. Mom gently lifted the angel from her nest of tissue, fluffed the skirt of the satin gown, and handed it to Dad.

Dad stepped up to the tree, carefully placed the angel over the top spike of the trunk, arranged the skirt, and then stepped back. The angel wobbled for a few moments, then slowly tipped drunkenly to the left. She ended up at about a forty-five degree angle to the tree, with the right side of her skirt lifted high by the trunk, and her legs exposed in a most non-angelic way.

"Well, that won't do," huffed Dad as he stepped forward to readjust the angel's position. He carefully straightened her out, spread out the skirt again, and stepped back. For a few seconds, it looked like she was going to stay put, but then she slowly tipped forward. This time, she ended up with her head balanced against the first branch of the tree while she gracefully "mooned" the front windows of the house. I could feel a giggle building in my chest, and I didn't dare to look at Donna for fear that we would both end up collapsed in helpless laughter.

As usual, Mom came to the rescue. She went to her sewing room and returned with a few strips of white satin ribbon. While Dad held the angel in place, Jim gently tied her legs to the top spike of the tree with two strips of ribbon, each ending in a lovely bow. The skirt was fluffed out once more, and this time stability was achieved.

"And now," Dad announced, "for the final touch. Donna, turn off the lights so that it's dark in here." Donna flipped the light switch as Dad plugged in a small spotlight set on the floor near the wall. The spotlight was aimed through a disk that was divided into thirds, each third being made of translucent plastic of a different color. The disk began to turn, clicking as each ratchet on the gear advanced, and the tree was bathed in a flood of blue light that gradually changed to green and then to red. The colored light had a unique effect on the angel: the blue gave her a frozen, icy look; the green produced a distinct "flu-like" appearance; and the effect of the red was a demonic cast that completely changed our angel's personality.

Dad sighed with deep satisfaction. "Now *there* is a Christmas tree!" He turned his attention to the empty boxes. "Mother, let's put these boxes away." They gathered them up and headed for the closet of their room.

The spotlight clicked in the background, slowly working its way through the changing wash of colors. The tree stood, perfectly straight, with its sparse, spiny branches sticking out at exact angles. The ornaments hung from the branches, looking very much like birds lined up along telephone wires. Or, perhaps more accurately, like rows of fat bats hanging from telephone wires. There was no tinsel, no sparkling, flashing lights, no bubble lights, and no strings of popcorn and cranberries. Our angel slowly changed from ice queen to plague victim to mad ax-murderer, while the spotlight ticked away like a time bomb.

Donna and I looked at each other, and then we both looked at Jim. He just shook his head and shrugged his shoulders.

"We *have* to talk to Mom about this," Donna said.

"Something tells me you won't get very far," replied Jim.

"But, she has to hate this as much as we do! We *always* have a real tree," I interjected.

"And Christmas trees should be green," Raymond added softly.

With a final disbelieving glance at the tree, we turned and left the room.

*   *   *

The next afternoon, while Dad was attending a Knights of Columbus meeting at the church, Donna and I ambushed Mom in the kitchen. We walked in together (effectively blocking any escape route), and Donna started by asking, "Mom, can we talk to you about something?"

"Of course you can, girls. What is it?"

"Well, it's about the Christmas tree…"

Mom paused for a second, and then turned to us and said, "All right. Tell you what—why don't we sit down at the table and get comfortable while we talk about this?"

We moved into the dining room and sat down. Ray slipped in from the living room and climbed into his chair as Mom asked, "Now, what's bothering you?"

"Is that *really* going to be our Christmas tree this year?" I asked.

"Well, yes, it is. It's all set up and decorated. Why would we take it down?"

There was silence for a few seconds while Donna and I looked at each other. Then Donna ventured, "But, it doesn't really *look* like a Christmas tree. I mean, we always have a real tree, and that one is pretty ugly, don't you think?"

"Well, perhaps it is a trifle gaudy, but it should work well enough."

"Oh, no, Mom. That thing is awful! And, the angel had to be *tied* to it like Joan of Arc at the stake!" I blurted out.

"And that light thing makes the angel look horrible," said Donna emphatically.

"And the ornaments look weird on it."

"It just doesn't feel like a Christmas tree. And it doesn't smell like one, either."

"It looks like something from outer space!"

"I think it should be green," ventured Ray.

Mom listened quietly while we voiced our opinions. When we finally ran out of derogatory things to say about the new tree, she looked at all of us and asked, "So, what you're saying is that it's the appearance of the new tree that you don't like?" We nodded in agreement.

She glanced around at us, and then continued, "Christmas trees, and ornaments, and lights and such are simply symbols of the season. They're fun, and special, but they are not Christmas. Christmas is inside each of us."

She paused again, and then seemed to change the subject. "Have you noticed how much more involved with the holiday your Dad has been, this year?"

"Yeah, I guess so," I said, a little hesitantly.

"No, Pat," added Donna. "Mom's right. He's been doing a lot more this year."

"And he's been a lot happier than I've seen him for several years," Mom said. "Now, you know how much your Dad loves surprises."

I giggled a little. "Well, he likes to surprise other people, but he's not so crazy about getting surprised, himself."

Mom smiled at that. "True. But, this year the new tree was his big surprise for the whole family. He's been excited and happy about it for weeks now, and that carries over into everything else he does. He's having a really good time this year. Don't you think so?"

We thought about it for a few seconds and agreed.

"Well, then, I agree that the new tree doesn't exactly fit our ideas of a Christmas tree, but it is just a symbol. I believe the packages will fit under it nicely, and it looks enough like a tree that, with a little imagination on our part, it should work quite well. Now, keeping in mind that it's Christmas, do you really want to hurt your Dad's feelings by grouching about something that he thinks is special?"

She glanced around at us, now using one of her "Mother looks" to full advantage. Humbled, we shook our heads.

"I didn't think so. Let's all reach down inside of us into what Christmas is all about, and then let's be kind and gracious about the tree. Okay?" She stood quietly, and went back into the kitchen, but I thought I heard her mutter under her breath, "Even if it is ghastly."

The rest of that Christmas season passed without incident and the sci-fi tree made it through the holiday just fine. The tree made encore appearances for several years, and came to be accepted as *our* tree. Mom, once again, had been absolutely right.

'Til Next Time...

Once again, the time has come for us to draw our story-spinning to a close, at least for now. We hope these tales have brought a smile or a chuckle to your day, and we thank you for once again spending a little time with us in Paxton.

As with our first book, we found that producing this one focused our memories, thoughts, and energies, and produced some thought provoking conclusions. Christmas has always been a treasured time for us, and we discovered (or re-discovered) that the value of the holiday had very little to do with gifts given and received, the amount of money spent, or whether our decorations and preparations outdid those of the neighbors. Instead, our fondest memories centered on our traditions and the renewed sense of peace and unity with our family and friends. The year-end holidays were a time of celebration governed by our hearts rather than by business or government.

Today, we hear many people tell us that they dread the holidays, and they speak of Christmas as if it is a painful chore that must be endured. How very sad that is, even though it can be somewhat understood. The media and merchants in this country have decided that we need at least a third of the year to prepare for Christmas, and they dutifully begin bombarding us with the holiday in early September. Please! The leaves haven't even turned yet, and Halloween is still two months away!

The barrage continues, though, with ads thrown at us on television, radio, in magazines and newspapers. Magazines run articles and features on gift giving, decorating, and special "gourmet" holiday cuisine, all of which emphasize the idea of spend, spend, spend. We find it funny that those "gourmet" recipes usually include at least two ingredients that are never found in a normal kitchen, and that the decorating tips for this year rarely use anything you were encouraged to purchase last year.

As the holidays come closer (say, mid-October?) the media treats us with articles about dealing with "holiday stress" and, inevitably, a few articles that point out the dangers of *not* dealing with that stress. They cheerfully inform us that the suicide rate increases every year over the Christmas holidays. At least they do offer a few hints for dealing with the stress that they have largely created.

Perhaps one of the best ways to deal with holiday stress is to relax a little about the holidays. Let's start a grass-roots movement to return to the fun and joy of the holidays, and to make them the celebration they should be.

Perhaps it is time for all of us to pause, take a deep breath, and say a collective, "Stop!" Then, as Mom suggested so many years ago, let's all reach down into ourselves to discover what Christmas is all about, and plan our holidays accordingly.

We don't mean to imply that we have all of the answers. Instead, we believe that you have all of the answers for yourself—you just need to find them. Revive some of your family's holiday traditions, or create some new ones of your own. If you need some ideas for getting back to basics, consider visiting a small town in your area. If you live within a reasonable distance of Paxton, you might consider going there.

Paxton still raises the huge town Christmas tree on the day after Thanksgiving, and the next day is the annual Christmas parade. Santa will be there for the children, the merchants will welcome you, and you will find a town full of friendly people. If you have the time, make a day of it. Start with the parade, then plan lunch at The Two Sisters Café or The Country Thyme Tea Room. (At Country Thyme, call ahead for reservations—the food is all prepared fresh daily and they need to plan amounts. The phone number is 217-379-4800.) You might want to sample one of the locally famous, hand-made pizzas at the 102 Market Street Bar and Grill, or try some country style fare at the Country Gardens Restaurant and Pancake House. (The portions are generous, and the prices are very reasonable.)

As you stroll around town, be sure to stop in at Hudson's Drug and Hallmark Shop, a virtual cornucopia of unique gift items and tasteful Paxton souvenirs sponsored by Pride in Paxton, a non-profit organization and member of Main Street USA. A visit to the State Street Mall will offer you a variety of shops featuring crafts and specialty items.

If your taste doesn't lean towards shopping, you might take a brief walking tour of the town. There are a number of beautiful historic buildings and homes sporting seasonal decorations. Be sure to buy a copy of The Paxton

Record for additional information about seasonal events, promotions and activities. While you are there, relax into the spirit of an old-fashioned Christmas.

We are planning to take some time off over the holidays to spend with our family and friends. After the first of the year, we will be back to work on our next book and will have it ready for you as soon as we can. Meanwhile, let us wish you the merriest Christmas ever, and all good things in the New Year.

Grandma's Best Ever Christmas Sugar Cookie Cut-outs[1]

1 cup sugar
1 cup (2 sticks) butter, softened
2 eggs
½ teaspoon baking soda
1 teaspoon baking powder
¼ teaspoon salt
3 cups all-purpose flour
4 tablespoons sweet cream
1 teaspoon vanilla

1. Sift together dry ingredients; set aside
2. Beat together sugar and butter until fluffy. Add eggs. Beat until creamy
3. Add sifted dry ingredients alternately with vanilla and cream, mixing well between each addition.
4. Chill dough thoroughly (usually overnight).
5. On floured surface, roll dough to 1/8" thick. Using cookie cutters, cut out cookies.
6. Place on greased baking sheet.
7. Bake at 375°F for 8 to 10 minutes, or until lightly browned at edges.
8. Cool thoroughly on racks.

Yield: Approximately 5 dozen cookies.
Note: Cookies may be frosted with basic vanilla frosting and decorated with candy sprinkles. If you prefer, sprinkle cookies with colored sugar before baking.

---

1. Page 71, *And a Chicken in a Pear Tree*

Basic Vanilla Frosting

4 cups powdered sugar
½ cup butter (or shortening)
¼ cup milk
1 teaspoon vanilla
Food color optional

1. In large bowl, beat butter and sugar together until creamy and fluffy.

2. Beat in milk and vanilla.

3. Add food coloring if desired.

Note: Store in refrigerator and keep covered to prevent drying. If frosting is too thin, you can thicken it with more powdered sugar.

Yield: 2 ½ cups

If you have enjoyed reading
*Merry Christmas from a Little
Town Called Paxton*
please share information about the book
and your reactions with friends.

To order additional copies call 1-877-288-4737
or
Go online at

www.iUniverse.com
www.bn.com
www.Amazon.com

It can also be ordered through fine
bookstores everywhere.

If you would like to learn more about the town of
Paxton, Illinois, visit their web site at www.paxtonil.com.

978-0-595-37295-9
0-595-37295-3

Printed in the United States
38034LVS00006B/364-435